What's Your
FREAKIN'
POINT?

Maximize the Impact
of Every Word You Speak

JOE CURCILLO

THOUGHT EMPORIUM LTD

What's Your Freakin' Point?
Maximize the Impact of Every Word You Speak
by Joe Curcillo

For information, contact:

THOUGHT EMPORIUM LTD

Thought Emporium, Ltd.
3964 Lexington Street
Harrisburg, PA 17109
www.ThoughtEmporium.com

ISBN: 978-1-73248-560-0

LCCN: 2018948875

Printed in the United States of America

To my wife and daughters.
"Yes, ladies, I will get to the freakin' point."

Preface

WHEN I STARTED MY legal career, I would watch more experienced lawyers in court. I had anticipated that they would possess the skills of an orator. I expected them to have focus, clarity, and appeal. I wasn't expecting legal arguments to be entertaining, but I thought that—at the very least—they would be understandable. To say that I was disappointed would be an understatement. I wanted to jump up and shout, *WHAT'S YOUR FREAKIN' POINT?*

I had learned much at Temple University about the art of advocacy, but entered the practice of law in 1985 assuming that I would learn more by watching. I quickly realized that the life-long entertainer in me had demands that were way too high. So as a green, newly admitted attorney, my journey of self-discovery as a speaker and presenter began.

I saw the good, the bad, and the ugly. I kept copious notes and honed my skills as a presenter. Along the way, I did great things, I did mediocre things, and sometimes, I fumbled. I learned from it all. (And, yes, I probably learned more from my mistakes than my successes.)

I spent my career exploring the Art of Advocacy as well as the Art of Presenting. Throughout, I worked hard to master the philosophical theories of argument and make them usable in everyday communication. As I prepared each legal argument and every jury trial, I diligently applied my ongoing education, and every day I asked myself, *What's your freakin' point?* This question dogged me as I tried to be relevant, informational, and believable in every word I spoke.

For all of us, the way we present our thoughts and ideas becomes integral to our success. By making our words more focused and organized, our message becomes easier to understand. When done properly, the process of planning each presentation will lead us on a path to greater understanding of our topic, ourselves, and our audience's needs. As you will learn in this book, the perfect presentation is a balance of those three areas of concern: logic, self, and emotion.

In the pages that follow, I will share with you the secrets of CEOs, managers, and entrepreneurs, the secrets that I learned along the way to building my dual careers as a litigator and an entertainer.

What's Your Freakin' Point? is a new edition of my first book, *Performance on Trial.* The prior edition was written for professional magicians and mentalists. In that work, the foreword was written by veteran Broadway actor Bob Fitch. Bob has worn many hats in his lengthy professional career. He counts twenty-seven Broadway shows and received Broadway's Burns-Mantle Award for Best Featured Actor in a Musical for his villainous portrayal of Rooster Hannigan in the original production of *Annie.* I was honored by his words in that foreword:

> *As an actor, I find that Joe's techniques are identical with the more sophisticated acting techniques, and yet the learning curve is so stimulating that you'd never think*

you are acting. You feel grounded throughout the entire book.

This book is part story, part courtroom drama, and part workshop; it's about acting the part, it's about communication techniques. It makes such sense that you'll want to apply his concepts immediately. He's very persuasive; the logic of his arguments is very clear, very powerful. No filler material here. It's a hard-hitting, practical treatise written by a very down-to-earth guy.

I first saw Joe at a performance workshop I gave. I didn't want to critique him. I just wanted to see more. As his acting coach, I am excited to see him share his theory of presentation with the business world. He puts great thought into every presentation. There are many layers to Joseph. He has a highly imaginative and mischievous mind. But he's got a serious and professional mind as well. This book is not just idle talk or pie-in-the-sky stuff. He is offering you the real work ... work from the inside out ... work from a professional.

It is with Bob's humbling praise that I offer this new edition to assist you as you build upon your past achievements, and I wish you much success on your road to making your own (freakin') point clearly and concisely!

GET READY
TO WOW THEM!

THE TIME HAS COME. Your nerves are on edge, your stomach knotted with anticipation as you step in front of those to whom you must sell. There's a lot at stake. Your next paycheck—maybe every paycheck for years to come—hangs in the balance. You pause in quiet reflection and review everything you are about to do. Everything that you have studied, learned, and prepared comes down to this. Your innermost self will be splayed before the public; you will be judged for your efforts.

Are you ready? Have you committed to memory the words that prove your competence and skills? Have you considered the variables? What if someone blurts out a question that you haven't anticipated—will you have the answer? What if one of your demonstrations is flawed or you make a mistake? Can you recover?

The crowd is attentive as you begin to speak, but they're skeptical. Can you hold their attention? Will they find it in their hearts and minds to observe and listen? Will they love you? Will they still love you when you finish? Will they accept your explanations and suggestions as they unfold before them? Will they believe what you ask them to believe, or will they reject your assertions and claims?

Will they maximize the concerns you seek to minimize? Will they minimize the concerns you seek to maximize? Will they suspect that you're hiding something? Will they spend the entire time trying to catch you in a lie?

You have spoken. All your meticulous preparation and reasoning was laid bare. Did you drive home every point? Did you nail every beat? Were you clear enough? Did your audience buy into the world that you created with your carefully chosen words? In the end, it is you alone who will be judged. Your efforts will be scrutinized, and your entire presentation and pitch will come down to the moment when you stop, pause, and say "Thank you."

At that moment you are powerless. The results are in the hands of the people you worked so hard to impress. Did they feel involved? Did they understand the message? Did they accept the world that you presented to them during your presentation?

You are done. There is no second chance; the moment has arrived. You await the decision. Will the jury find your client guilty of first-degree murder? Will an innocent man who looks to you for guidance be sentenced to death?

I am an attorney and my audience is the jury. If my presentations don't succeed, if I don't do every ounce of preparation, if I don't anticipate every eventuality, an innocent person may face a lengthy prison sentence—or death. The stakes couldn't be higher.

I have been a successful trial lawyer since 1985. I am also a professional stage magician and a *mentalist*—in other words, *I can read your mind.* (Not really; but sort of … it sure does look like it!). I play to packed houses and they pay me to do it. In the years that I've been battling in courtrooms and making things disappear, I've discovered—sometimes the hard way—that there are several skills and traits that set the superstars apart from those who just muddle through.

And do you know what? Those skills and traits are the same whether I'm practicing law or asking "Is this your card?" They help me persuade people to come around to my way of thinking and to *enter a world* that I've constructed in my head. In law, I present a world where my client is innocent. In magic, I present a world where the impossible becomes real. In either case, I have to convince people to see things my way—to enter my world, believe in it wholeheartedly, and act upon my suggestions. My career has been built upon giving people options, and then convincing them to see things my way.

Do you ever have to persuade someone to see things your way? Your boss, your spouse, a client, a committee, a boardroom?

Of course you do. Who doesn't? And the skills and traits that I use will help you, too, regardless of your career or calling. They can be learned, practiced, polished, and applied. They're as old as the philosophies of ancient Greece and Rome, yet they're right up to date and completely at home in the 21st century. In this book I share the theory of performance that I rely upon whether I am on stage or in the courtroom. These techniques have served me well in obtaining both favorable jury verdicts and vigorous applause. Using anecdotes, theory, and war stories, we will explore the parallels between the artistic and adversarial processes—the former primarily used on stage, and the latter in the courtroom (and sometimes in the boardroom). Yet there are aspects of each process that are applicable to the other environment, and that are also applicable to your own situation, whatever that may be.

Stick with me through these pages and we'll discover …

- How the classical art of Rhetoric and its five *canons*— Invention, Arrangement, Style, Memory, and Delivery—will help you build a better presentation.

- How Aristotle's persuasive appeals—Ethos, Logos, and Pathos—will help you win over the toughest crowds.

- How to hone your delivery to achieve maximum impact and the results you desire.

- How to select key people in your audience—board members, clients, or the general public—and tailor your words to their ears.

- How to use the art of storytelling to capture and hold your listener's attention.

- How to demonstrate your knowledge and expertise.

- How to emphasize your strengths and deflect attention from your weaknesses.

- How to manage your audience.

- The nuts and bolts of a powerful presentation.

- How to put it all together into one neat package.

Of course, you don't *have* to learn these skills. Many people don't, and they do okay. Do you want to do okay? Or do you want to do great? Read this book, apply what you learn, and you will take your career to a new level. You'll have more fun, you'll enjoy greater success, you'll have a bigger bank account, and (my favorite result) people will think you're smart. Sound good? How could it not? Go get a drink, have a seat, and turn the page...

CASE PREPARATION

AS A MAGICIAN, the final applause (or lack thereof) can feel like a death sentence or a complete acquittal. It can destroy me or it can validate me. My ego is at the mercy of the audience. To protect it, I have no choice but to perform as if my life depends upon it. Certainly, as a trial lawyer, I truly care about my client, but in my heart, it is always me on trial; that pressure forces me to be my best.

The courtroom is an adversarial environment, but in the performing arts, there is no visible adversary. Instead, the adversary that we face lives within us and within our audience: *doubt.* That hesitation which exists when we are asked for the very first time to accept the unknown is the enemy, and the enemy must be vanquished. Conquering doubt is the key to success, and we conquer it through education and preparation.

In late 2017, I watched a newbie lawyer argue a case before a judge. He had mastered his research; he knew his stuff. Unfortunately, the fear and confusion in his eyes as the judge began to question him was reminiscent of a small rabbit in the talons of an eagle.

The young lawyer understood the method and rule of law, but he was ill prepared for the judge's unexpected diversion. In show business, the interaction with spectators can lead us astray if we don't learn to control the moment through experienced fluidity. We must roll with the punches.

We must set out with a script that proves our power to create belief and entertain, and no matter what occurs, we must guide our spectators back toward the conclusion that we are wonderful. We must understand how belief is created, reinforced, and argued. We must know how to use all available resources to create our desired reality.

Every presentation can be understood in the terms of an argument. According to Webster's Dictionary, an argument is *a reason given in proof or rebuttal; discourse intended to persuade; the act or process of arguing; a coherent series of statements leading from a premise to a conclusion.*

An argument is not the throwing of dinner plates, getting a divorce, or fighting with a teenaged child. While those moments are responsible for some of our most memorable arguments, they are extreme examples. Our culture has attached notions of anger and enmity to the concept of argument, but at its root level, an argument is simply an attempt to do more than make a statement or an assertion. It is an intentional act or series of intentional acts designed to allow others to conclude or believe that what you present is true rather than false.

We must prepare our presentations, whether on stage, in court, in the marketplace, or in the boardroom, as a series of intentional acts focused upon our desired conclusion that the audience will accept us and the world as we wish them to see it—*our* reality. Your audience may not care what you believe, but they will care about what you *inspire* them to believe. Only when you believe fully in the position of your argument— when you have bought in completely and without reservation— can you expect to persuade others to believe in it too.

As a criminal-trial lawyer, I script every trial in meticulous detail. I study the facts and issues in the case until the intricacies are ingrained in my mind. I rehearse and practice each thought and phrase. Then, I walk into a courtroom, check my notes and script at the door, and become fluid. When we watch shows about lawyers on television, we see scripted dialogue and argument where, by virtue of the script, everyone knows what the next response will be and who will say it. In the real world, we must be ready for anything. Keeping a trial on your planned course is akin to herding cats. Just when you get a witness under control, opposing counsel acts contrary to your plan, or worse yet, the judge sustains an objection and you *must* move on without affect. Fear and weakness will cause a setback.

Your audience may not care what you believe, but they will care about what you *inspire* them to believe.

The script is essential, but we must have a built in GPS to bring our presentations back on course. While our outlines and scripts are a road map, we need to have the fluidity to alter the course around detours and other unanticipated road blocks.

Much as a lawyer calls each witness to prove his case, you must use each point you make to prove your power and skill. Each word you speak must contribute to the pool of evidence that supports the proposition or premise you seek to establish. All roads must lead to your credibility and believability.

You learn from the insight and reflection that occurs when you apply *your* thoughts to *your* actions.

The good news is that *your* audience is there, for the most part, by choice. In trial, the audience of jurors is forced under penalty of law to sit through the duration of the event. Talk about a tough crowd!

As a performing mentalist, I will also share my thoughts on how to create a magical world by better understanding the trial process and the theories of argument. Sound daunting? This information is anything but. Learning positive argument theory will give you an edge and give you the chops to inspire your audience to want to be "in your world," and accept your authority.

One more thing. As you read this book, please take the time to consider a Socratic thought[1]: *As you read, ask yourself, from time to time, what do you think? What examples come to your mind?* Your thoughts as you read are far more important than my words. You learn from the insight and reflection that occurs when you apply *your* thoughts to *your* actions. This book is about a mindset. I hope it serves you well.

---

[1] Socrates was an advocate of the proposition that inquiry and questioning stimulate rational thought and illuminate ideas. The Socratic Method of instruction relies upon the teacher assuming the role of inquisitor, and the student must look inside himself or herself to explore the available answers.

THE MAGIC OF RHETORIC

What Is Rhetoric?

GIVEN THAT I'M ITALIAN *AND* A LAWYER, verbosity runs in my veins. I badly want to give you a long, intricate definition of rhetoric and argument theory, but I'll spare you the ordeal and give you a short one: Rhetoric is "the ability to see what is possibly persuasive in every given case.[2]" So, for you, the presenter, each presentation should be laced with enough information and authenticity to support the propositions and "arguments" that you are making.

Marcus Tullius Cicero was a Roman political leader, lawyer, political theorist, and philosopher, widely considered one of Rome's greatest orators and prose stylists. In 55 BC, Cicero wrote:

Since all activity and ability of an orator falls into five divisions, ... he must first hit upon what to say; then manage and marshal his discoveries, not merely in

---

[2] Aristotle, *Rhetoric* I.2

orderly fashion, but with a discriminating eye for the exact weight as it were of each argument; next go on to array them in the adornments of style; after that keep them guarded in his memory; and in the end deliver them with effect and charm.

~ Cicero, *De Oratore*

Breaking this down as a roadmap for a great presentation, Cicero's *Five Canons of Rhetoric* are as follows:

1) **Invention** - Methods of persuasion; the ability to find the argument in any topic.

2) **Arrangement** - Structuring a coherent presentation and argument that your information is correct.

3) **Style** - Presenting the argument at three levels: Teaching, Persuading, and Entertaining.

4) **Memory** - Arguing impromptu; the ability to call upon knowledge from within.

5) **Delivery** - Making effective use of voice and gesture.

INVENTION

David Copperfield, one of the most celebrated magicians of our time, steps onstage before a rapt audience. He announces that they are in for a rare treat: He is going to learn a new trick tonight, right on that very stage, and he will reveal his working methods to the lucky souls assembled in the auditorium that evening.

He begins by pressing "play" on an ancient tape recorder, and the audience hears the slick-voiced narrator of an audio magic course that is clearly intended for young children. As if this weren't absurd enough, Copperfield suffers an epic misunderstanding with the instructor's very first words: when told to "find a bandana" the magician instead produces a *banana*. From there the situation quickly rolls downhill as, instructed to fold the bandana this way and that, Copperfield is soon left with a messy, mushy handful of pulp and peel, all the while struggling to maintain a cheerful, nothing-is-amiss smile. The audience roars its approval.

And yet ... every single member of that audience knows that they are in the presence of one of the world's greatest magicians. They know that this is all a put-on, a sham. But they buy into it. They accept Mr. Copperfield's version of reality as they watch him fumble with the wrong prop through an entry-level trick. They gladly enter the world that he has created. How does he do it?

At the outset, the premise of the effect is that this expert—this man at the top of his game—stands before his public and prepares to learn a new effect on the fly. The routine itself is a funny creation, but watching someone whom we know to be a master fumble through it is funnier because it is contrary to his expertise.

The voice-over, the props, and the sarcastically cheerful display of emotion work in harmony to build a level of comfort that puts the audience right where Copperfield wants them. We are at the threshold of his imaginary world.

Each step of the way, Copperfield draws upon our expectations and our thoughts like a series of dominoes falling in perfect sequence. In the end, as the trick climaxes, the relief, satisfaction, and joy make us realize that he has led us down the proverbial primrose path.

His flawless adaptation, organization, and use of his reputation and spectator emotions is presented and delivered with the skill we expect from a great presenter. We cannot help but be drawn into his world, and we find ourselves laughing at him, with him, and at ourselves. We enjoy the ride and, like it or not, we are drawn into his world. And through it all, Copperfield never speaks a single word.

Which brings us to the first canon of rhetoric: *Invention.* Invention is the ability to find the argument in any topic; the ability to identify the strengths and weaknesses of your presentation. The ability to see the situation from all sides is a learnable art. Step back from the point that you want to make and ask yourself, "What are the parts of my presentation that speak for themselves? What parts must I prove and what parts must I defend?" If you cannot see the weaknesses in your own presentation, you are doing yourself and the content a disservice.

When a client enters my law office for an initial consultation, I listen. From the outside, the interaction appears to be a one-sided dialogue. The client relates his story, I listen and, as needed, I elicit information. I have had initial consultations that have lasted for several hours, and I have offered very little information during the majority of the meeting. I am too busy gathering and learning.

Truthfully, I wonder what the client thinks they are paying for. I remember one of my first experiences with a lawyer. He asked me questions; I spoke. At the end of an hour, he suggested a four-sentence course of action. I remember thinking ... *and I paid for that?*

After that initial meeting, I realized that the lawyer had worked harder listening to me for one hour than I had during my entire eight-hour workday. In fact, the lawyer's *real* work and effort spanned the years before that meeting as he learned to listen; he had learned to see all sides of a situation. In future discussions, I realized that he had categorized the information I offered and identified each of the issues with laser accuracy.

When I listen to a client, my attention is focused on the presentation of the case to a jury. I identify issues and non-issues. I sort the understandable from that which needs exploration and explanation. I do this even if the case is a clear guilty plea. Assuming my client is absolutely guilty, and he hired me with the hope of getting a lessened sentence, I prepare the final argument to the jury. Once I successfully achieve this goal, I know that I can explain each and every phase of the case to anyone at any time. This full understanding is necessary to provide complete and comprehensive advice and guidance.

Do your best to find the right building blocks and put them together in the best possible way.

What works in law and magic also works in business. As you construct your argument, ask yourself: Have I carefully considered all the information? Have I extracted and categorized the key points? Have I evaluated how each component will integrate with the others? Just like a lawyer, you're building a case. Just like a magician, you're assembling a show. Do your best to find the right building blocks and put them together in the best possible way.

ARRANGEMENT

When I think of arrangement, I think of Hansel & Gretel dropping breadcrumbs as they walk through the woods toward the house made of candy. The points in your presentation should be orderly breadcrumbs that guide your audience from point A to point B. It is best to assume that the starting point is the knowledge level of the least knowledgeable listener. By doing this, you will allow everyone to follow your presentation. The least knowledgeable will not lose you, and the more knowledgeable will listen to a review of what they already know; then they can follow you gracefully as you enter new intellectual territory.

The audience must be able to follow your path with ease and precision knowing that they have not lost their way. It is up to you as the presenter to guide your listener and assist in their understanding of each point before you move on to the next. You must explain yourself sufficiently so that each person understands, but more importantly you must make the presentation interesting—or should I say *entertaining*—so that they will want to listen and follow you.

The more entertaining your presentation, the more readily your audience will follow your words. The information should flow in the same way information flows in a story. Each piece of information must be introduced and then built up. Each point must logically lead to the next. If you tried to talk about Gretel pushing the witch into the oven without first telling the audience that Hansel had been imprisoned by the witch, the story is one of murder rather than of a sister saving her brother. The information should flow so that each new idea makes sense.

Throughout my career, I have watched many lawyers make disjointed points. They stand in front of a jury pointing out all the flaws in someone's case or pointing out all the strengths in their own, in a disorganized fashion as if they are throwing darts at a board. This random approach doesn't provide listeners with a sufficient roadmap. When an audience gets lost it's because the speaker is disseminating information without having charted his own course.

Without giving due consideration to the arrangement of your presentation, your efforts will not be entertaining, and your information will not have a strong foundation.

The more entertaining your presentation, the more readily your audience will follow your words.

Build Your Foundation

Take a few moments to consider a typical conversation in your own life. Imagine a situation where you tell someone something that you want the other party to believe. The information is part of your knowledge, and it is accepted as part of your reality. You now want to share this information, and you want the listener to believe and accept your words. Either you naturally provide a basis for what you have learned, or you answer questions from the listener to allow them to process the information and judge its credibility. Build a foundation that allows the audience to drop their guard and trust you, and dare I say, be entertained by you.

You may say, "In this morning's *USA Today* I read…," or "On CNN this morning, I heard that…," or "I was reading a treatise on the sexual proclivities of the African tsetse fly, and…" In each case, your intent is to give the audience a foundation upon which to base acceptance; such is the nature of argument. You provide the source to add to your own credibility.

As a trial lawyer, it was my job to convince a jury to deliver the verdict as I requested it. When I was a prosecutor I asked for a guilty verdict. When I was a defense lawyer I asked for a not-guilty verdict. This was the end goal. Throughout the process of the trial, it was incumbent upon me to present evidence in an orderly fashion so that the jury could follow me to the journey's desired end. When I challenged evidence from the other side, I did so clearly and precisely so that the jury continued to understand. In the times when I had the opportunity to address the jury, I reminded them of their importance in our system of justice. And all of this was done in a cohesive understandable fashion. If it were not cohesive, minds would wander, the imagination would run rampant, and distrust would ensue.

At the end of trial, when I addressed the jury for the final time, I reviewed all of the evidence with them and remained consistent in all that I said and did. The desired result was never a surprise. I reminded the jury where I was going, and I followed them down the path as I urged them forward. If I delivered all of the facts and information to them appropriately, I did not need to lead them. They knew the decision that I was going to request, and it was my job to provide logical support for my request as we moved forward. I wanted them, with my urging, to arrive at the decision before the words left my lips. It was a coup when I realized that they already saw the picture that I was painting.

In one particular case, I had the opportunity to represent a man charged with arson who I truly believed to be innocent. The weeklong trial culminated with the testimony of an arson expert who explained that the origin of the fire was accidental. I watched as the jury listened intently to his instructional and educational tone. He explained his position with clarity and order; he was friendly and knowledgeable.

Once the jury accepted my expert, I called my client to the stand. My client was a small educated gentleman who had emigrated from Bombay. He spoke softly, with the fear of an innocent man charged with a crime. By putting him on the witness stand after the expert, his personality shone as he allowed the jury to find comfort while they incorporated his version of events into the conclusions of the expert. Without the client's testimony, the jury would have been educated, but never would have been at ease in rendering a verdict of not guilty. Giving them a reason to feel safe in their verdict was the goal. They liked my client because he was authentic and made sense.

When I closed for the jury, several jurors looked behind me and stared at my client. They did not do so with disdain, nor did they look at him as a guilty man. They looked at him as if they understood the pain that he was suffering. While my request for a not-guilty verdict was necessary for the sake of closure, it was clear that a number of the jurors had already made their decision. In fact, after finding him not guilty, the jury was dismissed and wandered the courthouse. My client, now proven innocent, called his father in Bombay with the good news. The jury foreman asked if he could also speak to my client's father. Taking the phone, he apologized for what his son had been through and praised my client as "a very good man." Not only did the jury do as I asked, but they did it with complete acceptance. It was their decision.

As a result of the presentation, the jury felt as if they were a part of my client's life, so much so that one of them felt that a message needed to be conveyed to his family as if they were long lost friends. The shroud of guilt that my client wore when he entered the courtroom was lifted, and the jury felt welcomed into his world.

Today, the skepticism that we possess about being told what to do, or about being persuaded into something by another, leads us to be very wary of those seeking to influence. Why is it that we do not simply do what others tell us to do? It's because we resist anything that contradicts the assumptions that are lodged in our subconscious minds. Unfortunately, much of what we think throughout our lives is created by those around us. We may be holding on to tried-and-true life systems that have been successful in the past, thus we are inclined to reject anything new without first seeing proven results.

To be properly persuaded, people need to feel a sense of trust, safety, and comfort. Therefore, great consideration must be given to the fact that you must care about your topic, and that you want to provide your audience with the knowledge needed to accept your message.

When the relationship between the presenter and the audience is built correctly, their skepticism and resistance will fade; they will listen.

This process is the same whether you're a magician, an attorney, a businessperson, or an entrepreneur. The goal is to draw your audience into your world, the argument is the process that gets them there, entertainment is the diversion that makes both possible.

Whatever your occupation, it is essential that your presentations *entertain*. Whether your audience is in the theater or in a corporate conference room, if you bore them you will lose them. You can't bring people into your world if they aren't paying attention. Like it or not, if you make presentations, you are in show business. Successful entertainment is about connecting with the audience.

I'm not talking about being comedic or performing song and dance, but I am suggesting that you present with the audience in mind. A skilled juggler or a beautiful singer will fail if they only worry about themselves. But, when the performer knows how to do what they do so well that they can focus their attention on the audience, they will be entertaining. Whether you are teaching, selling, or managing, the people to whom you speak must be made to want to listen to you. Once you know your material, turn your attention toward delivering it with a focus on the listeners rather than on your slides or written material. Be yourself. Do not be an extension of the material.

Once you get their attention you have to keep it, and each step of that process becomes a breadcrumb that leads the spectator along *your* path. You must make each breadcrumb palatable so that the transition toward the desired goal occurs naturally. People will listen when they are emotionally, factually, and visually entertained by you.

STYLE

Once you make a point, be sure you give the audience sufficient time to accept and adopt your argument. As a magician, the argument may be that the chosen card was "lost" in the deck. This can be proven by the magician shuffling the deck, but it may be proved more efficiently by allowing the spectator to shuffle the deck.

If the magician guards his cards and allows no one else to touch or shuffle them, one may assume that he is skilled in the handling of cards. If, however, the person chooses a card and shuffles, and the magician never touches the deck, the level of mystery increases greatly.

Each step of your presentation must educate your audience and provide additional proof of the assertions you make. I am not speaking of the education that we dread when we think back to school, but education about what you are doing, why you are doing it, and what you want your audience to believe. You are teaching the audience truths about *your* reality, the reality that you want them to believe.

When I speak to a jury, they need to understand the law. If I were to delve into every nuance, their understanding and comprehension would deteriorate. When understanding deteriorates, boredom and confusion follow. With boredom and confusion come loss of attention. The key to educating your audience is this: Ignore that which you want your audience to ignore, and focus on that which you want them to understand. The thoughts and ideas in their heads must be clear.

The balance between the need to educate your audience about what you want them to know, the need to convince them, and to entertain them, is delicate. Treat it with the same care and consideration with which you would treat a decision of personal importance.

MEMORY

Memory isn't rote memorization. It involves the ability to spontaneously remember and recall that which you have learned. Think of impromptu comedy when the performer must instantly call upon inner reserves of knowledge and expertise. The improv comedian is confronted with a situation and must humorously work with the information at hand to move the audience to laugh. This is achieved with an open and positive mind, and the ability to react effortlessly as new information is gained. In sports, we talk of muscle memory. The muscles in a pitcher's arm react according to their training because the muscles "remember" the trained actions as they are called upon. Be in the moment and allow your brain to react based on its past learned behavior.

In ancient times, the Romans taught that memory was essential to great argument. Argument—or actually rhetoric itself—was a means of proving that one had stature. The goal was instruction in the ability to speak, think, and deliver with respect and confidence.

When you watch a great entertainer interact with the public, pay close attention to the ease with which they interact with and flow throughout the situation. As you watch an improv comic respond to the seemingly absurd reactions of their partners, watch the speed with which they reply: A veteran performer will conjure a rejoinder with barely an instant of thought. Or, on the other side of the coin, watch as a politician fluidly responds to a reporter's questions without meaningful reflection.

Several years ago, my mentor as a professional speaker, Charlie "Tremendous" Jones, hired me to speak to an insurance company after the audience had endured a long day of classes and training.

A few days before the engagement, Charlie asked me to stop by his house. We spoke about many things, but not about the booking. As we walked across his yard, he asked when the event was scheduled. I told him it was in two days and I was nervous. He told me there was no need to be nervous because *"Either the words are in your heart, or you are not ready."*

The night of the event, I arrived at the hotel with ample time to spare. I did a sound check, identified difficult architectural spots in the room and, most importantly, I ensured that my notes were behind the podium. I went to the lobby for a cup of coffee. I sat back and thought through the several modifications that I had made to personalize my presentation and found composure. I was in my happy place; my moment of Zen was underway.

I made a decision. Charlie had booked me, and he wanted me to speak from the heart. Therefore, if I did that and failed, he would be good with the result. Right? I chose daring over logic. Could I do what he asked me to do?

I took my notes out to the car and locked them inside. When I returned to the room, my stomach descended to its normal altitude as I went into an "I'm ok, you're ok, this sucks" frame of mind. I walked outside, sucked in an inordinate amount of air, and ran back to the ballroom. I successfully feigned professionalism, all the while suppressing the fear of the three-year-old within, and I told the CEO I was ready when he was.

The CEO introduced me. I rose, stood before the microphone, and spoke. For one hour, I spoke coherently and competently. Well, actually, I don't remember what I said, but they laughed when they were supposed to, and they applauded loudly at the end.

Upon conclusion, I walked over to the CEO and thanked him. He said I did a fantastic job and assured me that he would have me back to speak at another event. I had survived.

I often think of Charlie's advice whether I am on stage, in a courtroom, or even when I teach in a classroom. All of the knowledge we learn and all of the information we acquire is worth nothing if we don't have the courage to take off the training wheels and pedal as hard as we can. Your heart and mind will remember what you have to do. Prove you are a professional by drawing from the skills you have learned. Allow your instincts to be honed by an education based on skills, not presentational crutches. Allow your presentation to show the listener that you are talented, professional, and, dare I say, magical. Remember who you are. That is memory.

Follow your instincts.

DELIVERY

The most important thing for an orator to master is "Delivery. Delivery. Delivery." The next chapter is entirely devoted to delivery. It is that important.

ARISTOTLE ON STAGE

IN 1995, I WAS booked to perform magic at a company Christmas party. Between Thanksgiving and Christmas of that year, I performed thirty-two children's parties and ten adult parties. During that same thirty days, I tried, and successfully prosecuted, a five-day-long fraud jury trial. To say the least, my brain and body were fried. Between the trial and the shows, not to mention travel and preparations, I spent about eighty hours performing and on stage during those thirty days. The final show of the season arrived, and I finished show number forty-two. The five-week "hell season" was over. [3]

The audience applauded as I took my final bow. I was a success. Or was I? The client's employees came up to me to discuss the show. Every comment was positive. It was exciting.

I asked several people for their names and jotted their comments on index cards. (I am a promotional obsessive; you should be, too.) I stuffed the cards neatly into my breast pocket. Once the show cases were packed, I sat behind the wheel and reviewed the cards. I put them down. Then, in the

---

[3] The thought that the number 42 might hold special meaning as the answer to life, the universe, and everything else did not escape me. *Thank you, Douglas Adams.*

quiet of my van, I reflected on the comments. Something was wrong.

Every trick meant something to someone, the show flowed well, and everyone laughed. What more did I need? I kept flipping through the cards.

Suddenly, the problem was clear and all-consuming. I realized the audience didn't like *me*. They enjoyed my tricks— but they didn't enjoy Joe Curcillo. On the heels of a great show, I sunk into a world of disappointment.

The next day, I promoted my bunny to a house pet. I took a sabbatical from the stage.

During my hiatus, I resumed a position as a trial advocacy instructor at Widener University School of Law. The teaching caused me to re-think the trial work that I had also taken for granted and I again studied trial law from an academic perspective. I began to see similarities in performing magic and trial law. One of the most significant parallels was that Aristotle became my instructor in both careers, as well as in everyday discussions and storytelling.

The three aspects of effective argument advanced by Aristotle have endured for nearly twenty-five-hundred years. I see his three categories of focus in every type of presentation and art regardless of your or my field. They are *Ethos, Logos,* and *Pathos.*

Ethos is the essence of your character. It is your personal appeal, your authenticity. Logos is the intellectual appeal. It is the logical factors or the truths upon which you build the world you wish to "sell:" your knowledge. *Pathos* is the emotional appeal, that which appeals to the wants and desires of the audience; your human connection.

Let's strip away the Greek labels of Aristotle for a moment and simply look at your presentation as a construction project. The ethical appeal is you as the builder of the presentation. The question is, are you capable of building the presentation, and does the audience believe that you are capable of handling such a project? If the audience believes in you and accepts you for who you are, you will appeal to their sense of *ethics*. If the audience thinks you're ill-equipped or bumbling, you are off to a bad start. Always be prepared to start your presentation by being well versed and knowledgeable in your topic. Only then can you be truly authentic.

Like any construction project, once the builder has been selected, the next step is to build the foundation and the structure. This is the *logical* appeal. Just as the ironwork, brickwork, and carpentry hold the building together, all of the facts, information, and details that you share about your topic satisfy the intellectual need of the listener to understand.

And then there is the *emotional* appeal. This is where the architect comes in. The builder can build the strongest and most durable building, but it will hold no one's interest unless it is appealing. The architectural details are what make a building fascinating and appealing to the viewer. The same is true of your presentation. The architectural details of your speech or presentation are the bits of humor, the interesting slides, and the manner in which you present that make it all interesting.

Now that you've seen how the pieces fit together, let's back up and examine them in a little more detail…

ETHOS

Let's begin with character. Every one of us plays a character whether we realize it or not. Life casts us in roles. Many of us would agree that the version of ourselves that our coworkers know is not the same version that our families see at home. At work we play a role, a version of ourselves that heightens some aspects of our personalities while diminishing others. At home we show alternative sides of our personality and play a different character. We unconsciously play these roles; we do it without thinking. When it's time to argue, to present, to persuade, you must learn to *consciously* play a role. You must have a role to successfully perform, entertain, and convince. There are no exceptions. Understanding who you are is the essential ingredient in authenticity.

In my early years as a trial lawyer, I would morph from one great trial lawyer to another in the courtroom. I changed personalities just like jumping from stone to stone to cross a stream. My personality was several different characters, and the journey never led back to being myself. The inconsistency made it difficult for juries to accept "me" as being convincing.

I knew the result was fatal to my goal of being effective in the courtroom, so I had to change my patterns and redefine myself. I did this successfully, and subsequently I taught my methods to law students during my time as a professor.

I asked my law students to list every character trait that they believed they possessed. Then I encouraged them to talk to family and friends, and to ascertain the character traits that *they* saw. When this self-evaluation and external input was completed, they were asked to do two more things:

- Reconcile what they see in themselves with what others don't see in them.

- Determine what it is that they want others to see.

Then the final phase: Decide which character traits they will take into the courtroom, and which traits they will check at the door. Once this is completed, only the traits that assist in producing positive results make up their in-court character.

What part of you gets the best result?

Start by forgetting your professional role. Don't think about being a manager, a salesperson, an entrepreneur, etc. Let go of that role. Then, think about what you do that makes people smile. *What is it that you are doing when you receive the approval of a stranger? This person could be your next customer; don't you want that reaction again?*

Highlighting and deleting character traits from your persona list requires work, but it is essential because it is what defines *who* your audience, your customers, and your colleagues see, and whom they will be asked to believe.

There is one unbreakable rule: You must be believed to be accepted; therefore, you must NEVER make up character traits. Only work with what you already possess. You can enhance minor traits, or minimize major ones, but never invent a trait that isn't already within you. Some of your traits will be downplayed, and some emphasized, but in the end, you are you. Embrace it and act with confidence.

Unless—yes, lawyers do make definitive statements then declare exceptions—you are willing to consciously work on the trait until you can successfully adopt it and call it your own, twenty-four hours a day, seven days a week.

The way that you do what you do will always define who you are to the viewer. Seek to distinguish yourself. Your character and message must be consistent and must work together to move your audience to the conclusion that you are who you purport to be.

Sit back for a moment, pause and reflect upon how you appear to others. Who do people see when you speak? Generally speaking, what perception do you create when you are "on stage?" Are you a high intellectual who talks over the heads of the audience? Are you friendly and cheerful? How do people treat you when you are done speaking? Consider asking others how they feel you come across on the dais, and be willing to learn from any criticism and praise.

Without consistent character, your personality becomes a distraction that disrupts your flow and confuses your ultimate message. If you change your personality, demeanor, or overall attitude every time the audience gets comfortable with you you're going to force them to reconsider whether or not they like you. Their mental process will then be stuck in a rut, and they'll be distracted from your message. If all your proof falls on unfocused minds, you will convince no one that your presentation should be accepted, and you will only occasionally achieve the results that you seek. Occasionally isn't good enough.

If they love you, they will enjoy watching you eat lunch. They will accept everything for which you stand. Make them love you.

LOGOS

Your audience is *not* stupid. Period. The human mind wants explanation and clarity. But more importantly, we want our minds entertained.

When a movie begins, we normally know that the hero will not die. We know that, through all the tension and all the explosions, Rambo will live on. And, in the *Terminator* series we know that, in the end, Arnold is not dead. However, in all these movies, we watch for ninety-plus minutes and enjoy the ride. The reason is simple: We want to see what the hero will do next. The storyline engages us; the energy entices us.

We like to see the cool weaponry in James Bond movies. We like to see what Q will create next, and in the backs of our minds, we struggle to discern the line between the weapons that exist in fantasy, those that exist in reality, and those that may exist in the future.

There is just enough truth within these fictional stories to give us a basis upon which to build our own conclusions. We look for what we *know* to determine what we will now *accept*.

Consider the *Rambo* movies. We accept the argument that these characters could be real because we accept that our special forces are extremely well-trained fighting machines. While we find his combination of skills to be unlikely in a single individual, we want to believe in the possibility that such a superhuman being *could* exist.

When a presenter stands on stage, the audience wants to be entertained; the educational component comes in as a close second. The music, the introduction, the write-up in the company newspaper, and prior reviews all give us an idea of what to expect. When you give a sales or boardroom presentation your audience *still* wants to be entertained even though they may not realize it themselves. Once you set the tone, you must deliver. Give the audience what they expect. Entertain them.

If a magician walks on stage and pulls silk from his hand and does nothing more, then it is at best a flourish. If the audience is first provided the opportunity to see his hands empty, curiosity is satisfied, and the intellect is happy. Thus the waving of the hand in a relaxed state allows the audience to see it is empty and the mind will conclude that "the hand is empty." This is because the watchers have been given an opportunity to conclude that all is as it should be.

In magic, the subtle glimpse of an empty hand is a better argument for empty hands. The soft casual action does not scream, "My hands are empty!" If a magician tells you his hands are empty, red flags go up, and the desire to confirm the truth becomes a focus. The audience doesn't become as suspicious, because the conclusion that his hands are empty is reached by the audience with their own intellect based upon what they observe. A conclusion someone reaches on their own is a much stronger position than a conclusion that is forced.

People will resist a position that is forced upon them. Skepticism becomes a major defense mechanism that fights against the possibility of deception. Sure, some people will be sucked into a street con because they want the challenge, but most need to be soft-pedaled and lured into a situation where they will surely face deception. When people are provided sufficient information to reach their own conclusion, they are much more likely to accept what you want them to believe.

Education and learning are phenomenal co-pilots that allow us to take the audience to our magical place. Knowledge and information are the precursors to the logical choice. If people are provided sufficient information to make an educated choice, they will do so freely and comfortably. As a presenter, you will need to share the facts, data, and other information that supports your conclusion. The information you share will allow their logic to accept your conclusion when you present it.

If you give the audience enough acceptable and "reality-based" information, the logical choice will be easier for them to make. Accordingly, you may then effectively control the decision-making process. The details you deliver make your message more palatable.

In the business world, especially in sales, when you demonstrate your knowledge of a client's present situation, you also define the status quo within the context of your argument. Just like the magician pointing to his hat and saying "this is real," you have provided a foundation and a frame of reference for the proposition that you're about to make or the product that you're about to sell. And, just as the magician produces a rabbit and brings you into his world of magic and wonder, you bring the client into your world when you describe the benefits of your product and how it will improve or simplify the status quo that you defined. This is the world that you see. Make them see it, too.

Do you give your audience the information to choose the world you want them to accept? When you present, do you rush into your conclusion or do you first provide a factual basis to support it? How do you allow the details to engage your audience so that they are more willing to accept your position? Do you lead the audience or do you force information onto them?

Present the facts using the manner of delivery you chose, and the audience will follow you to your conclusion.

PATHOS

After a jury trial for burglary, I was sitting in a local diner with Denny, the defense attorney; I was a prosecutor at the time. A woman approached us and stared. We acknowledged her, but she shook her head and did not speak. I asked, "You were our jury foreperson today, weren't you?"

"Yes. Why are you two eating together?"

I simply responded with a polite but terse, "We got hungry. Would you like to sit down?"

She replied with a slight stammer, "But you two are here together. You are eating and talking and . . . We deliberated for an hour, and . . ." Then, looking toward me, she continued, "You won. We decided that in ten minutes. We spent the next forty-five minutes discussing how much you two hated each other."

Denny laughed. "In the courtroom, he is a pain, I hate him. Everywhere else, we're the best of friends."

The juror walked away in a daze. Watching us joke and laugh over our plates of chicken and waffles jarred the reality she created because of our "in-court" personas. We were both warriors. We both fought for our beliefs. We were both unwavering in our commitment to our duty.

What she saw was a battle: two samurai fighting to the death. While we thought we were both respectful and cordial in court, the jury interpreted our actions as hate for each other.

The jury had been, by their own emotions, pulled into the world they chose to believe. It certainly was not a world we intended, but it worked to my clear advantage.

If you give presentations or speak before crowds I hope you're in the habit of making video recordings of your work. When you do, also record the audience. The ability to watch the audience and yourself will help you acquire a sense of how the audience is reacting to your every move.

Ask yourself who is in the audience. What type of people are they? Are they there because they want to have a good time? Are they there because they want to learn? What are their shared experience levels? How much do they already know versus what they need to be taught? Are they there to see you? What does the audience already know about you?

When you speak to an audience as your authentic self, the real you will shine through. You may actually care about your audience, but if you don't take the time to provide them information, they may feel as if they are neglected. If they do not have sufficient experience to stay in step with you, they will feel as if they have been left behind.

It is imperative that you do not confuse the image you believe you are conveying with the image being received. Ensuring that the images are one and the same requires considerable thought and self-evaluation. Allow your personality to shine through. Do not become bogged down in your presentation or they will never truly get to know you, because the material will stand in the way. Be yourself and be authentic.

The Legendary Hypnotist

In the early 2000s I had the pleasure of spending time with Ormond McGill. He was in his eighties, a gentle old man who was both kind and polite; he was just damned lovable. He had spent his life creating his own legend as the world's greatest stage hypnotist. When a spectator walked on stage, he touched her head and asked her to sleep. She nodded off instantly. His reputation as a master hypnotist preceded him. We *saw* his ability to hypnotize, and we *knew* of his stature. He relied heavily upon both to draw in the touched spectator. His charisma was magnetic in every sense of the word. He knew very well how to focus his character, knowledge, and emotional appeal into a simple touch.

His reputation initiated the emotional argument long before the curtain rose; it's what warmed up the audience, just like the overture that plays before the show begins. The composer creates an overture to generate enthusiasm and set the mood before the performers take the stage. In Hollywood, there is typically an opening scene to set the tone: An innocent victim is killed, a funny situation unfolds, or an event occurs to take us to the place the director and/or screenwriter wants us to be before the movie begins.

The Philadelphia Lawyer

The first time I observed a jury trial, I watched a powerful and famous "Philadelphia Lawyer" talk to a jury and argue to save his client's life from the death penalty. I remember reaching the conclusion that each statement he spoke was said with confidence. He exuded respect for the jury and gave them rational, logical reasons to allow their emotions to prevail. Interestingly enough, he never called upon their emotions directly.

As an attorney, it was not permissible to openly tug on the heartstrings of the jury. He could only rely on the facts and the law. There was no room for emotional decisions, but the courtroom that day was full of unspoken emotion. It was inspiring. His ability to connect with the jury was incredible. I wanted to do that so badly that, shall we say, "The rest is history." Both the jury and I credited him with greatness because he lived up to his reputation; he benefited from my emotion and expectation.

Both the Legendary Hypnotist and the Philadelphia Lawyer created emotional appeal through their stature in the community. Nevertheless, both men had to start somewhere; neither had the advantage of audience emotional appeal during their first shows.

What do you do to begin your emotional appeal? Is it in your handshake? Is it in your smile? Is it in your small talk before getting down to business? These seemingly insignificant moments are anything but as the success or failure of all that you do could come down to the emotional connection that you make with someone the very first time that you meet.

I love watching young magicians perform. When a nine-year-old girl walks on stage on *America's Got Talent*, the emotional appeal is not earned; it is freely given. The audience wants the child to succeed; the hearts and souls of the viewers pour out to the child. But you're not a nine-year-old kid. You have to earn your emotional appeal.

A great place to begin is in your opening. *What is the mood set by your opening words? Do you talk and warm up? Do you give the audience a chance to warm up to you while you take a moment to warm up to them?*

Anyone can take someone out to dinner on a first date, and anyone can have a rational discussion, but if you want to make it past dessert, you need to find that emotional connection. We have all been there. How do we show the date that little glimmer of our heart and soul? Or, how do we show our "sensitive side"? Slowly, we open up and share pieces of our lives, moments that we believe will help the other person see the real us. When we are engaging in an argument, we want to be believed and accepted. If we express a hint of humanity, people want more. People naturally want to explore our vision once we send out a teaser that appeals to their sense of curiosity. On stage, this can be accomplished with an anecdote, a joke, or in many cases, a facial expression, a gesture, or our posture.

Once we open up and are authentic, people will be more willing to trust us. Look at our first-date analogy. How often have you heard someone say, "He was a cold fish, I couldn't get through with a chisel." Wouldn't it be nice to hear, "I saw something in her I liked. She was interesting. I want to get to know her better."

Will your audience want to take you on a second date?

**Once we open up and are authentic,
people will be more willing to trust us.**

ETHOS, LOGOS, AND PATHOS IN HARMONY

As you can clearly imagine, the character, intellect, and emotional appeals all mesh and, when used effectively, they overlap and the lines between them blur.

From Rags to Riches with a Book and a Chicken Sandwich

In the mid 1990s, as I sat in the lobby of the Hotel Hershey to decompress and relax after a grueling two-day leadership presentation, a small, unassuming gentleman in his seventies greeted me with a gentle southern drawl. I knew he had attended the seminar, so I rose to shake his hand. He asked, "I understand you live locally?"

"Yes, I do…," I replied.

"Have you read any Horatio Alger books?"

I admitted that I had not.

"They are wonderful!" he continued. "They are inspirational." He described Alger's rags-to-riches tales and how hard work, determination, courage, and honesty were his core topics—and that those traits were the keys to success.

He said, "I love to pick up old Horatio Alger books. Are there any good used bookstores near here?"

I told him that there was a great used bookstore about 35 minutes away. "We need to go there now," he said, because there is "so much you can learn from those stories." He continued to share his excitement. It was contagious. My curiosity was at its height.

He smiled. He knew he had my attention.

Before I knew it, I had agreed to take my new friend to the used bookstore. After settling into his seat, he finally introduced himself: "My name is Truett Cathy."

The founder and CEO of Chick-fil-A was in my passenger seat. Really? If I had realized who he was, I would have agreed on a dime. But then I wouldn't have learned how simply persuasive an interaction could be.

When I think back on that day, I remember how his excitement became my excitement. He so deeply wanted me to love Horatio Alger that I changed my plans for the afternoon and went book shopping.

I now realize that this short interaction was the perfect presentation. Truett's southern charm and candor made him the perfect builder; his discussion with me began with his inner charm and credibility. It kept my attention. His methodical explanation of why I needed to read Horatio Alger books was pitched on the heels of a leadership seminar that was frankly way above my pay grade at the time. I knew I had a lot to learn, and he presented me with a credible foundation and a logical structure that led me to conclude that I needed to do what he said. The pathos, the architectural detail of his presentation, was nothing more than his incredible feeling of excitement about what my future held if I did as he asked.

Three hours later, and with two large bags of books each, we drove back to the Hotel Hershey. I was in awe of how he made me feel about meeting him; not in awe of Truett Cathy, CEO of Chick-fil-A, but in awe of the small, unassuming, sincere, seventy-something southern gentleman who used *ethos, logos,* and *pathos* to get me interested in hundred-year-old books.

The Perfect Marriage of *Ethos, Logos,* and *Pathos*

Your audience will accept your position and follow along with you if your delivery is well orchestrated. You must look at each point that you present, and put "you" in it. You have no option but to carefully choose words and narratives that you can adapt to your character. Only then can you connect with your presentation, make it yours, and successfully create the emotional appeal that your audience desires.

The ability to trust is, at its core, an emotional decision. With all the proof we can gather, and with all the emotion we can create, our goal of acceptance will fail if we do not have a character that the audience can embrace. The *Logos* and *Pathos* can die if you forget or never discover your inner character.

I once watched a magician named Peter Samelson present a routine that began with him telling the tale of his father's snow globe. It warmed our hearts. The emotional appeal was obvious. But there was also a logical appeal that was not so obvious.

As he began, he thanked the audience and talked about how we all have lifelong memories. All eyes focused upon him, the storyteller. The theater became intimate as we were emotionally and intellectually pulled into his story; we all related to our own memories. We wanted to feel good, and he made that happen. We connected to the story he told because we all possess memories that make us smile. Our minds embraced his story as our hearts felt his warmth. The story was simple and it is one we freely accepted as true because we could believe it; we saw his story. We freely chose to allow emotional involvement, because we were logically secure with the facts and we liked him.

The ability to trust is, at its core, an emotional decision.

Then, when snow originates from his visibly empty hand and fills the theater, we watched with complete and total amazement. We accepted the magic and forgot everything else. The warmth of the words he spoke were in direct contrast to the snow we witnessed. The perfect marriage of *Ethos, Logos,* and *Pathos* enchanted us.

Whether you are a comedic performer or a serious presenter, whether you are a magician or a psychic entertainer, whether you are an attorney or a salesman, a manager or a CEO, you must put you into your presentation.

Every presentation begins with your preparedness. When you walk on stage, enter a boardroom, or stand before a casual group, keep in mind that you should always maintain balance. Setting aside all of the ancient Greek philosophy, the three areas that you need to master to be a great presenter are:

1. Know yourself,

2. know your material, and

3. know your audience.

Once you achieve a level of comfort with these three areas, you will find balance in your presentation, and your audience will connect with you in the words that you speak.

A well-structured presentation, like a well-structured argument, must contain balanced proportions of *Character Appeal, Intellectual Appeal,* and *Emotional Appeal.* The measurements change from person to person and from topic to topic. For some of us, success is a matter of patience and practice. For others, it will flow as if it is our birthright. The majority of us will find that the art of performance and the art of rhetoric require a balance of our natural skills and our learned techniques. The challenge will always be finding the balance that is right for you.

THE LAWYER'S THEORY OF THE CASE

Create Interest

Lawyers are trained to plan a case based on a clear and concise theory. That theory needs to be designed to make the case easy to understand. It has to tell the jury that following you is the best alternative. If a lawyer can offer the jury a simple, understandable position, they will follow because any other path would be more difficult.

In the business world you should consider how you will make the information and your overall presentation interesting and inviting; design your presentation so the audience can follow you.

When you deliver a presentation, you share your knowledge and your perspective with the audience. What you teach them may be something new that they need to learn, or may be something old of which they need to be reminded. Either way, you introduce to your audience information that is a part of your world, but not necessarily a part of theirs.

You should consider how you will make the information and your overall presentation interesting and inviting; design your presentation so the audience can follow you.

To get someone to embrace the information that you share, and to accept it as true, your presentation must invite the listener to voluntarily choose to be a part of your world. It must hold their interest. Your presentation style is what creates the interest.

Follow me—for a moment—into the world of a magician. The magician creates a world that isn't real. Accordingly, the magician asks the audience to be a part of something that is— at inception—fantasy.

The magician, as a performer, has an obligation to bring the spectator with him into his "world of illusion." Thus, the goal or argument of the magician must lead to a resolution where the performer and the spectator stand together in spirit. A successful balance of proof, belief, and entertainment will win the audience.

The necessity of bringing the performer and the audience together in the same world is the basis of entertainment. Moreover, if the audience is entertained, then they are the benefactors of the presenter's success.

The magician as a performer and designer of his show has an obligation to provide the audience with sufficient information to make the magical world both believable and enchanting.

The information the magician presents must be about the audience. When a magician is focused upon the tricks—the illusion he creates—the performance becomes about his ego. There is never anything magical about someone else's ego. A business or sales presentation is no different. When the presenter is focused on how much he knows about the topic, the audience—even though it may be impressed—isn't going to find any joy in following his discussion. The audience will not follow.

A successful balance of proof, belief, and entertainment will win the audience.

Early in my legal career, I had the opportunity to present testimony in a homicide case from a well-recognized expert in forensic pathology. Dr. Mihalakis was frankly one of the most intelligent individuals I had ever met. He lived in a world where he derived all of his information by doing autopsies and analyzing dead bodies. This was not a world that anyone else in the courtroom had ever entered. Certainly, no one on that jury had ever experienced the doctor's world.

In order to understand his testimony, the jury had to understand his highly technical and sometimes utterly shocking business. When I called him to the witness stand, I asked his name. He said, "I am Dr. Isidore 'Jerry' Mihalakis." He then asked the judge, "May I step down from the witness stand so that the jury can better understand me?" The judge granted his request, and the remainder of his testimony was a conversation about pathology, autopsies, and information he learned from the body of the deceased.

By stepping down from the witness stand, he placed himself at the same level as the jury. Recognizing that the jurors had never heard testimony like they were about to hear, he conversed with them and taught them everything they needed to know to find his conclusion truthful.

As smart as he was, the jury embraced him and listened to every word he said, because at no time did he treat them as anything less than equals. He understood extremely well that his presentation meant nothing if the jury did not keep up with him and learn from him. If he had an ego at all, it was not present in the courtroom that day. The information and the way that he explained it to the jury allowed them to enter his world of forensic pathology. Despite the shocking nature of the testimony, Dr. Mihalakis connected with the jury and his world became their world. They understood him, and more importantly, they were entertained by his charming personality He knew his objective was to be educational and entertaining: he kept the jury engaged.

Before your presentation, you should be able to clearly state your objective. Know where it is that you want the audience to go, and what it is that you want them to learn from you.

Once you have established an objective, add to it this phrase:

"... entertain the audience, and connect with them so that they will feel engaged."

For instance, your main objective may be to teach the audience about a new widget being produced by your company. In that case, your objective would be, "Teach the audience about the exciting new widget we are producing; *entertain the audience and connect with them so that they will feel engaged.*"

If the human mind is not provided with sufficient structure and information to bridge the real world with the "new" world of the magician, then fantasy fails and enchantment is not achieved. The audience will never connect with the magician, and the audience will never connect with performer.

A skilled presenter puts his audience first.

In the business world, the knowledge is real—it is not fantasy, but it is a new world for the listeners. You are sharing an idea or concept that requires the listener to accept your words as true. We have all attended seminars and conferences where our primary focus is our search for distractions. Where is our newspaper? Is our laptop charged? We do this because we as an audience have been conditioned to believe the speakers will not pull us into their world, and we will need something else to do.

A skilled presenter puts his audience first. By putting the audience first, the presenter becomes a "welcomed distraction" and the audience will pay attention.

Sometimes, our nerves get the best of us. We worry so much about what we're going to say, all of our attention is on our presentation rather than on the people we are seeking to engage. We forget to connect with the audience because we are lost in our own thoughts.

An effective presenter guides the audience from their world into the world she creates. It may be a sales presentation where you want the audience to accept your business proposal, or it may be a management meeting where your world requires the adoption of a new fiscal policy. In any situation, if the audience is not invited, put first, and welcomed into the world created by the presenter, they remain mere observers.

When the audience simply observes, they are more inclined to question what they see and feel. On the other hand, when they get swept up in your world and become a part of it, they will buy in completely and give it their all. The presenter cannot expect to get the audience's "all" into his or her new world unless he first enters *their* world and leads them by the hand. You must give your all if you wish to receive *their* all. Make your number one priority a connection at a human level.

Francis Bacon observed that man has a "desire of learning and knowledge, sometimes upon a natural curiosity and inquisitive appetite; sometimes to entertain their minds with variety and delight; sometimes for ornament and reputation; and sometimes to enable them to victory of wit and contradiction; and most times for lucre and profession."[4]

The presenter must commingle every word, action, and thought to create a moment in time for the audience to share;

---

[4] Francis Bacon, *Of the Proficience and Advancement of Learning, Divine and Human.* (The First Book, 1605).

he must create a sensory experience that makes the listener feel involed in the presentation. When a magician suddenly reaches into a hat and pulls out a rabbit, there is no magic. It is just a rabbit. On the contrary, if a magician takes the time to ponder the situation, reflecting for a moment to consider the emptiness of the hat, the audience will ponder and observe the empty hat with her. The pause and the showing of the empty hat gives the audience time to join the magician in her experience. If the audience is provided an opportunity to digest what is happening, they will more likely than not follow the entertainer's lead. It is only at this point that the rabbit can be produced and the entertainment value of the production can be appreciated by all, including the magician. The element of time combined with observation is what creates the mystery.

Likewise, in your own business, when introducing new concepts or important information, it's important to pause for a moment and let it sink in. Let your listeners absorb what you've said. Only then will they be prepared for the next piece of information.

When you take a position and push that position upon someone, the reaction will likely be rejection. When you slowly and gradually allow the other person to understand your position or information, they will become more willing to voluntarily accept what you say. Worry more about having a conversation than about simply speaking. The audience may not be conversing with you as you speak, but you can imagine that they are discussing the topic with you. Imagine the conversation as part of your presentation and create a balanced dialogue.

Allow the audience to be enchanted with your presentation. Use your personality to create a magical experience that others want to share. The creation of enchantment is dependent upon the acquiescence of the spectator; they have to want to be enchanted. If you provide satisfaction for their concerns and imagined questions, and thereby lessen their curiosity, they will be more willing to allow all their senses to be satisfied. Belief will be the result; or, at the least, they will be willing to believe. Effectively, the audience will surrender their world for yours.

Use your personality to create a magical experience that others want to share.

Ultimately, you want your audience—whether it is one or one thousand—to put down their phones, close their laptops, or simply stay awake. People will do that when they feel that they are being provided an opportunity to escape the everyday. People will pause and listen if they believe that what you are going to teach them will make them a better person or, at least, a more educated one. But they are never going to believe in your ability to do that unless you are willing to look at yourself as a tour guide leading them from their current existence into the world that you desire to create for them.

Think back to the most interesting teacher you had in school. If you are like most people, the teacher that comes to mind is the one who seemed to care most about you as a student. It is the one who took the time to help you connect with the material. The course was much less intimidating, because the world the teacher was leading you into was one where you knew the teacher would be there to assist.

In late 2017, I was talking with a top CEO who was preparing to address an audience in the pharmaceutical industry. He knew that the audience would consist of two diverse types of people: half of them would be pharmacists and science nerds, and the other half would be the salesmen and party animals who brought in the money. He had to connect with both types.

We reflected on his school days, and I asked, "Who was the greatest teacher you had in college?" Without missing a beat, he told me it was Professor Smalls. He described how Professor Smalls could connect with the class in an almost magical way. Some of the students were focused on the fact it wasn't the weekend and they couldn't party. Others were there to learn. But Smalls connected with both.

How did Smalls connect with both types of audience members? He did it by being human. He didn't try to impress them as a stuffy professor. Smalls understood his audience. He knew that not everyone in the room was there to learn. He recognized the difficulty of the material, because he never lost sight of the fact that he was once an uneducated college student. Acting as a tour guide, he made the information interesting, and through a humorous personality, he made learning fun.

As we finished our conversation, I simply reminded the CEO that when he spoke to his audience, he should be just like Professor Smalls. Don't talk down to the audience, and don't talk over their heads. Talk with them, share with them and make the information you are presenting fun to learn.

People feel more welcomed when greeted by open arms, a hug or a kiss, than when greeted by a terse "Get in here." Excitement and enthusiasm must be communicated with your performance to create the mental welcoming hug needed by the traveler entering into a new place. Otherwise, the travelers will remain where they are in their own world. If they cannot find security in a new place or your "new" world, they will keep the status quo, and stay where they are. In a later chapter we will discuss how to move people into your new world of thought and action, but for now, remember that you must be welcoming to keep their interest.

When Was the Last Time You Bought a Mattress?

A few years ago, I finally accepted the inevitable: My mattress wasn't going to last forever. It was shot, and I had to get a new one. I walked into a store and was greeted by a salesman who immediately suggested that I needed to lay on a bed connected to a computer which would determine my body type and how I slept. It was then, after making me watch a video, that the computer performed calculations and spit out a sheet of paper.

The salesman looked it over and told me that the best mattress for me was... wait for it... the top-of-the-line high-ticket model right next to his desk. He then highlighted all of the benefits of coils, the memory foam hybrid, and all of the individually wrapped and compartmentalized springs that were the purported solution to my perfect night's sleep. Knowing nothing about mattresses, and frankly, not even knowing what kind of mattress I was currently sleeping on, I listened. What followed was a complete barrage of facts and information that went way over my head.

I realized that all of the information that they provided was nothing more than logic clouded by details that were incompatible with my vision of Dreamland. I had no reference point. Their world was not inviting, so I did not buy a mattress.

The next morning, I walked into another store, and a man named John greeted me and welcomed me to his store and asked me my name. He proceeded to give me a brief history of how long he had been in the mattress business as well as a brief history of his company.

John was so pleasant that I decided to cut to the chase and ask, "Can I tell you why we are here?"

He gave me an odd look and paused. The obvious answer was that I was there to buy a mattress, but he made no such assumption.

He simply said, "Yes."

I said, "I'm not here to buy a mattress. I'm here to have you convince me why I should buy from you."

We chatted for a bit and he assured me that if I was not happy with the mattress, he would facilitate an exchange. He followed that promise by telling me, "I have been here for eighteen years, so you will call me if there are ANY issues sleeping on the bed that I recommend." He paused and took out pen and paper saying, "Here is my mobile number. Call anytime."

I chuckled and said, "I haven't bought anything yet…" He cut me off and said, "Who cares? I'm your mattress guy."

I hadn't committed to a sale, but I knew who he was, I knew who his company was, and I knew that he was focused on making me happy. He created trust, and I felt good. Feeling good is what I expect from dreams, not thoughts of coils and springs and other technical things. He was a gracious host there to welcome me into his world. He captured my attention, trust, and respect; I felt like I mattered, and his world was a safe place to explore. He was the guy I would buy my mattress from.

How do you feel about people you meet each day? Aren't you more comfortable with those who are more open? Do you feel at ease with the people who relate to you? Do you feel at ease with one who exerts the energy to create the simple gesture of a smile? What makes you feel welcome?

You will find that the more you incorporate the experiences of your audience, the more they will feel invited by you and your presentation. When you are able to share experiences that you have in common with your audience, they will relate to you. It is very difficult to connect with someone if you have nothing in common or if they do not seem to respect you or care about you.

Your authenticity as you deliver the message will make you the authority of the information that you share.

If the world you create is an inviting one, the audience will be more willing to test the waters. A cold, commonplace presenter who merely uses his audience members as observers of his intellect may impress with his skill, but he can never lead them into a new world. And he will always be just another talking head that no one remembers.

Everyone who has visited the Grand Canyon remembers its majesty. Everyone who has seen the Louvre remembers all the beauty within. Rarely do we remember the name of the guide who led us on the tour.

When you take a spectator into your world, it is paramount that they remember the world you create *and* that they remember you as the guide who did not lead them astray. Your authenticity as you deliver the message will make you the authority on the information that you share.

PART TWO

YOUR PRESENTATION "ON TRIAL"

*Extemporaneous speaking should be practised [sic]
and cultivated. It is the lawyer's avenue to the public.
However able and faithful he may be in other respects,
people are slow to bring him business
if he cannot make a speech.*
~ Abraham Lincoln

6

JURY SELECTION

Know Your Audience

Jury selection is a tedious process. The attorneys scrutinize potential jurors and eliminate those they deem inappropriate; each lawyer weeds out undesirable candidates to select an "audience." There is no glamour, thus the process rarely makes it into *Law & Order* television shows.

The operation is, by its very nature, a de-selection process. Jurors are asked questions, their background questionnaires are reviewed, and they are observed by the attorneys. Some of the "on the spot" evaluation and assessment is based on gut instinct and intuition. The lawyers then seek to remove unacceptable jurors.

Jury selection is the first opportunity for the lawyers to meet the prospective audience and, while the attorney is focused on assessing potential jurors, the jurors are assessing the lawyer who, therefore, must make the best possible impression. During jury selection, the goal is to keep those jurors whom we think will like us, and get rid of those who seem disagreeable to us.

Another distinguishing feature is that the jury, once selected, has no ability to walk out. They must remain as spectators for hours, days, and sometimes weeks under penalty of law. Their applause is the verdict. If you fail as an entertainer, applause is light. If you fail as a salesperson, you don't make the sale. If you fail as a defense attorney, someone gets convicted. A bad performance may translate to a lengthy jail term—or even death—for your client.

THE GOLDEN RULE

From the moment you arrive at the venue, you must recognize that every face you meet could later be your judge. A gruffly treated doorman may turn out to be your lighting technician. The person you ignore on the elevator could be the front-row-center seat at your presentation; the only face you will see surrounded by an otherwise dark room.

Once, during my early days as a trial lawyer, I had truly put my best foot forward during jury selection. As the final twelve were seated in the jury box, their eyes and bodies told me that I was the better liked of the two attorneys.

Each juror looked at me as if to acknowledge their support of the "nice young man" chosen to represent the government. I felt relief; the world was good.

The next morning my hopes and energy were high. As the jury filtered through the door from the jury room, their smiles reinforced my positive mental attitude at the dawn of battle.

Suddenly, I noticed a flurry of glances among the jury. Eyes rolled and bodies fidgeted in their seats. As I stood to begin my opening statement, a veil of darkness fell over the courtroom. I delivered my opening to a jury I did not recognize. Were these the same people who were the source of a positive evening and a good night's sleep on the eve of trial?

They seemed inexplicably annoyed. Words fell from my mouth, but my mind reeled with questions. I could not figure out what I did wrong.

On a positive note, the bad attitude continued through the defense attorney's statement as well. I found a modicum of solace in the apparent "mutual defeat" in the opening gambit of the war that lay ahead.

Thankfully, the judge ordered a recess at the conclusion of the statements. I retired to the law library to collect my thoughts.

In the leaded-glass window that overlooked the parking lot I saw the reflection of a trooper, my key witness, over my shoulder. I assured him that it would all be fine: "You're my next witness, and I know that we can bring them back—we make a good team."

He replied, "Not this time, Buddy."

I turned and stared. His face did not have the confidence that I had known from our past. He cast his eyes to the floor and said, "I was in a rush this morning and I cut off jurors one and five. I stole the last parking spot. I think they hate me."

Act One was rough. Act Two was now impossible.

Your presentation begins the moment you make the first human contact and continues until you return home.

Over the next two days I worked to rebuild my bond with the jury, and the trial ended as I had hoped.

This memory has lingered with me for years. As a performer, a one-hour show would have ended without recovery. The audience's discomfort with my assistant—the trooper—would have surely stifled the applause; I would not have been accepted. The first hour, in which I struggled to "perform," because I was full of confusion and doubt, was remedied by my performance over the next few days. Every time I walk on stage to perform as a mentalist, I recognize that the first few moments are all I have to win over the audience; there is no time for recovery.

Your presentation begins the moment you make the first human contact and continues until you return home. As soon as you thank the audience after the last presentation, your next presentation begins.

Everyone you meet could be your next audience. Live well.

You have the benefit of knowing the audience is up front. Use that opportunity to gather information about them and find out who they are. What are their concerns? What are their needs? Knowing their education level will give you an opportunity to know how you have to approach that audience.

Knowing their cultural and socio-economic status will give you a glimpse into what is important to them. The more diverse your audience, the more you will be able to disseminate in a variety of ways to reach each and every person.

If it's a corporate audience you can gather this information on the internet. Or you could simply ask questions. If you are one of the lucky ones who get to speak within an organization where you are employed, you will have firsthand knowledge of what to expect when you walk before them.

The more you know about the audience, the better you will feel when you speak. Keep all you know in mind and speak to the audience in a way that they can embrace.

For instance, if you are speaking to an audience that consists of salesmen, find out what products they sell. The more you learn about the products the more you will be able to relate and deliver a message that they can connect with. If you are speaking to a group of executives, conduct a few interviews to get the pulse of what they need to hear. When possible, ask what is expected of you. When you are asked to present, the person asking you will have a vision of what they believe you need to cover. Ask. When you want to know how much knowledge your audience already has on your topic, ask. Questions and answers will define the way you relate information and the scope of the information you present.

You are there for a reason. Do not hesitate to find out what that reason is before you walk into the room.

OWN THE ROOM

If your audience will assemble in a particular room, make the room yours. If you can get access to that room prior to speaking, spend some time there. As a trial lawyer, it was not unusual to find me writing documents and preparing for trial in the actual courtroom in which I would try the case. It made it feel like my room. Today, when I do a presentation, a show, or a keynote, I will go to the venue—sometimes in the middle of the night—just to spend time within the four walls. The more time I spend in that room, the more it becomes my room, and the more comfortable I become in that venue.

Whether it is the audience or the room, you need to own your presentation. The more you know in advance, the easier it is to establish ownership and control.

FIRST IMPRESSIONS

When a lawyer begins jury selection, he introduces himself to the jury pool. Through simple introductory questions, the lawyer—if he uses his time wisely—can give the jurors a glimpse of what he is made of and of who he is.

Several of my friends are professional speakers. In fact, I'll go further than that: they are *legendary* professional speakers. Each of them makes it a habit of mingling with the audience prior to speaking. At first, I thought their socialization was a courtesy—an opportunity for the crowd to mix with the giants. Over time, and having had many opportunities to accompany them on their engagements, I realized that they were selecting their jury. They were feeling the pulse of the audience, sizing up each individual they met. Then, once on the dais, they took multiple opportunities to personalize the presentation to a few key people whom they met beforehand, and effectively, an audience of hundreds was personalized.

I once watched a speaker hug and bond with one individual that I classified as an obnoxious blowhard or potential sycophant. Yes, this audience member rubbed me the wrong way. I remember thinking "This guy is irritating. I hope I took my blood pressure medication."

Later, I sat in the hotel lobby listening to Mr. Blowhard tell everyone who would listen about the great message that he'd heard that evening and the power of the speaker. People were listening.

I chuckled as I realized how the preshow socializing had solidly won over this spectator long before the microphone was switched on. A few moments of preshow meet-and-greet created a first impression that resulted in extreme loyalty that would lead to long-term advertising. This spectator felt special, and now he wanted everyone else to share his special feelings.

Preshow meet-and-greet can work in just about any situation, but even if you don't have the opportunity, there are other ways to "work the room." If you've ever spoken before a group, large or small, you know that there are listeners who are tuned in and enthusiastic about your message, and there are those who will never unscowl their faces or uncross their arms no matter how polished or sincere you may be. As in magic and the law, find those who are receptive and play to them. Convince your skeptics and they will help you convince the unconverted.

PICKING THE AUDIENCE

In my early days as a prosecutor, I allowed a nicely dressed young man to remain on my jury. At his young age, I was impressed with his respect for the court. He was wearing a suit and tie. He was clean cut.

During the trial, he seemed to be interested, but he was not as focused as I would have liked him to be. In fact, to my dismay, I noticed that he had connected with defense counsel. He was alert when my opponent spoke. I toned down my presentation to speak to his "young mind." I did not want to lose a single juror.

Convince your skeptics and they will help you convince the unconverted.

After the closing argument, I watched respectfully as the jury left the box to begin deliberation. The nice young man was wearing work boots. Work boots? With a suit? I realized at that moment that for the last day and a half, he had been wearing the same suit. A new suit with work boots. A new suit that I suspect he bought just to get on a jury. Was it for the $7.00 a day? Was it to get on the jury to be somebody? Or, worse yet, to *do* something?

Ultimately, I learned he was there for a purpose. Other jurors came to me, after a verdict could not be reached, to tell me that he was the lone holdout. He told the jury at the beginning of deliberations that he would "never convict," and that "I hate this whole system."

Suddenly, the dichotomy between the new suit and the beaten work boots became clear. He was there to disrupt the process. His attire was designed to allow him to fit in so he would be able to get on the jury, and once on the jury, his mission was to rebel. Selecting such a juror was not a mistake I would make a second time.

Once. *Only once.*

What have you learned from your past performances? How many times must you tell a joke before you realize no one is laughing?

Don't Let Me Be Misunderstood! The Seven Types of Listeners

As you prepare to communicate, educate yourself about your listeners. Begin by sizing them up. Prioritize your audience; customize your message and delivery. Determine what types of listeners you're speaking to, then stop, think, and formulate a message (you might have to customize it on the fly!) that will strike at their hearts. Look around the crowd; observe the various people and how they act. What types of listeners are they?

As you consider the following list, think of people in your life. What types of listeners are they? Start communicating by thinking about how each individual is best addressed.

1. **The Active Listener** will hang on your every word. They will take in your message and listen attentively. They often show signs of response—either physically or verbally—to reassure you they are listening. The active listener will also be the first person to verbally give you feedback to assure you they understand. This is the Holy Grail of listeners.

2. **The Inactive Listener** is the speaker's worst nightmare. This listener truly allows the words to flow in one ear and out the other. Commonly, the inactive listener is far away in another place daydreaming or solving other problems. This listener is not really listening; they are not present. They may simply be waiting to state their position without even hearing yours.

3. **The Selective Listener** waits to hear what they expect to hear, or to hear what they want to hear. A selective listener only hears what's necessary to formulate a counter argument or may filter your words until he feels like he has achieved a minimum level of comprehension.

4. **The Rushed Listener** listens only as much as is needed to get the gist of what is being said. Then

they can transition comfortably into an inactive listener.

5. **The Defensive Listener** is arguably a subcategory of the selective listener. The defensive listener focuses on avoiding pain. Someone who is fearful of being criticized or rejected may only hear those words and phrases they feel they must defend against. Thus, you will be speaking to a selective listener in self-defense mode.

6. **The Eager-to-Please Listener** will give you signs of affirmation and support, but their only goal is to please you. Accordingly, they become a selective listener who sifts out those things they must do to make you happy. The message gets lost in their eagerness to please.

7. **The "Uneducated" Listener** is not a listener who is uneducated in an academic sense; this is a listener who is uneducated in the subject upon which you are speaking.

Don't Ignore Body Language & Appearance

As you deal with people, pay attention to their physical behavior and be aware of the message that you communicate with yours.

One single action or behavior—standing alone—may not mean what someone thinks it means. Everything must be taken in context. Watch people to understand their verbal and nonverbal cues. As an example, scratching the head is a signal that someone is confused. We can all picture a monkey scratching its head as it ponders a banana. It's almost as if they are trying to stimulate their neurons to work, and it's perfectly normal. But, keep in mind that if someone scratches her head repeatedly, it may not just be dandruff. Don't get caught up in the intricacies of reading body language. Watch everything and pay attention to the totality of the circumstances. If you are in doubt as to what a listener is thinking, ask her.

Individual actions must always be considered together with all available information. Learn from every person you talk to and, when you engage in an important conversation, you will be much more ready because you will be able to listen as second nature. You will know more about how to talk to them and how they will respond.

When someone holds their thumb the middle of a clenched fist that person may feel a bit distressed. If this happens, back off a little and let them relax. When someone holds their chin, this could mean curiosity, but it also may mean that the person feels insecure. In either case, be ready to address the various concerns people have. Even if you are right that this one person is insecure, someone else may be confused, so provide security and clarity in the remarks that follow.

Lastly, people will relax their arms when they feel open and comfortable. This is always a good sign. It means they are comfortable with you. When I see this happen, I think to myself, "don't blow it now. This is where you want to be."

This Is a People Business

Charlie "Tremendous" Jones always reminded his listeners, "You will be the same person in five years that you are today except for the people you meet and the books you read." We learn equally from both people and books.

Allow every person you meet and every book you read to inspire you to learn more about people, yourself, and the content of every presentation no matter how small.

Every time I perform, in or out of court, I learn something about people. *This is a people business; we need to learn from people as well as from books. What do we think when we meet someone? How do others react when they meet us? What did you learn from the last person you met?*

As I said at the beginning of this book, your thoughts as you read are more important than my words. Allow every person you meet and every book you read to inspire you to learn more about people, yourself, and the content of every presentation no matter how small.

THE OPENING STATEMENT

Storytelling and Presentation

The *Opening Statement* is the first time the jury gets to hear the story. First they hear from one lawyer, then the other. Each lawyer gets an opportunity to tell his or her version of the case. The opening is a statement. It is not meant to be an argument. As a matter of fact, in court, the opening is not legally allowed to contain argument. There are no challenges or a rebuttal, the presentation is merely an opportunity to provide the jury with a road map; the jury is given an overview of the case that lies ahead. It is an introduction.

The reality of a jury trial is that the twelve-member jury is there to make a decision. They know this is their obligation, and they sit ready to pick a winner and, by default, a loser. Experience teaches that the decision process has, for a vast number of jurors, already ended after they hear the opener; they already know how they want to decide. Studies reveal that although the jury is told by the judge to reserve all decisions until the end of trial, their gut instincts take over and they make up their minds. So, if the jury has already "jumped to a conclusion," why try the case? And, since you are obligated to proceed, what do you do?

The answer to both questions is, *You came to do a job; do it.* When a magician appears at a venue, the audience does not believe he has magical powers, but he does the show anyway. Why? Because he is the entertainment and he is obliged to deliver an entertaining performance.

Take a moment to imagine that no matter how good your presentation may be, the audience will pass judgement on you before you share 95% of what you have to say. If you stumble onto stage, are you going to quit and walk off? If you lose the board of directors in a three-minute opening remark, do you run away and resign? No, those are not viable options.

As you walk on stage, or face the jury, or prepare to address the board, your audience waits to be convinced. How do you take on this task? Where do you begin?

Simple. You begin powerfully, and you tease them to make them want to hear more. Before you walk on and start to speak, get your head in the game. Focus on why you are the presenter and trust your instincts to deliver. After all, you are prepared, and you know your material better than anyone in that room.

The first time I appeared before the Pennsylvania Supreme Court, I called an old law school professor for last minute advice. He simply said, "Don't be intimidated. You are prepared. Imagine that the justices know nothing. Deliver well and they cannot hurt you."

**Focus on why you are the presenter
and trust your instincts to deliver.**

As I began to argue my case, a smile rushed to my face as I saw seven ferns on the bench. I was successful. And, by the way, when I later appeared before the U.S. Supreme Court, I upgraded them to rhododendrons. That day, my biggest concern was whether Chief Justice Roberts would say my name correctly. He did. It is all a matter of having your head in the right place and opening strong.

OPEN STRONG

Your *Opening* is the dust jacket of your entire presentation. Not only must the audience be given an overall sense of who you are and where you are going, but they must become excited about looking beyond the cover; they must want to open the book. You must establish yourself and the desirability of being inside your world.

A movie trailer is assembled from the movie footage to entice us to see the movie. The trailer is meant to catch our interest, hold our attention and suck us in. That is what I do in my opening as a lawyer, and that is what I do in my opening as a performer. I want the jury, or my audience, as the case may be, to want to join me on my journey. If I can keep the jury or the audience with me each step of the way, I stand a much better chance of getting the decision or applause I want.

Any argument is easier to follow when it is spoon-fed to the listener one piece at a time. A book is easier to follow when it flows. Being on stage is the same experience. In preparation for the journey, the audience must be given direction. Your opener is a statement of direction. It sets the pace, the direction, and the spirit of your presentation.

Begin by introducing yourself. There must be something in your introduction that tells people who you are. It must be a reflection of you. Make sure that the introduction lets people know what your credentials are, and that those who have been part of your world are better for it.

A good introduction might include your experience as a presenter, companies you have worked with, and resume items that qualify you to stand in front of a particular audience. That information is great, but above all, make sure that your introduction makes you seem interesting and compelling.

A magician may begin his show with a flash of fire and smoke as he appears. Yes, this looks cool, but the reason for the action is that it draws all eyes forward. When you go to a concert, the band may begin with a song that everyone knows—or forgot that they knew—and the audience is drawn into the concert because they remember why they came. That opening song may not be the biggest track they have (they'll probably save that for the end), but they'll start with a song that people can relate to and that makes them feel like they're in the right place.

James Bond movies open with the bad guy hunting 007 in bravura chase sequences. He always endures some harrowing ordeal and ends with an exciting recovery. The opening tells everyone that this man does not flinch at the sight of danger, and that he's just so cool. It gives the audience a feeling of excitement knowing what is coming next. Your opening words have to tell people that you are going to rock.

Be James Bond. Let them know who you are and hit them with a statement that entices them to hear more. Make them want to journey with you. It may be a story that encapsulates the essence of your message. It may be a joke that lets them know you are going to be entertaining as well as educational. Or it may be a challenge that you know you will meet that makes them want to see proof or want to watch more to see if you fail. But you won't because you are prepared. Right?

A FORMULA FOR STORYTELLING

You opened. What do you do now? You tell your story.

Whether you are going to tell your story with words or actions or both, you simply begin.

No matter what story you tell, you *are* the story. Do not escape completely into a robotic script. Ultimately, the story must be a masterfully constructed blend of the story and you, the credible entertaining storyteller. Thus, while you need to present a solid, flowing chain of events, you must not allow yourself, as the vehicle of the message, to get lost in the midst of your presentation.

Prior to walking in front of a jury, I think of the jurors as a blank slate. I imagine that it will be up to me to decide *for them* how they will think. Whether it is true or not is irrelevant; it's my imagination. In my imagination, I will paint the picture, I will color in the outline, and they will love it.

Your opening words have to tell people that you are going to rock.

When I am teaching law students, lawyers, or CEOs, I use my Story Color Model™ to explain the necessary mindset for effective storytelling:

> **C**larify your thoughts.
> **O**pen your mind.
> **L**isten to your instincts.
> **O**bserve your audience.
> **R**ehearse.

CLARIFY your thoughts, and be sure they are organized. Ensure that you have a complete understanding of what it is that you are about to do. Not only must you know your lines, but you must also have a firm grasp on what you are *physically* going to do. Where will you stand? How will you stand? How will you use your hands, and what slides or demonstrative aids will you use?

Once you have imagined each word and each action, be prepared for whatever may come next. **OPEN** your mind to everything around you. By keeping your mind open, you will be more fluid as the presentation progresses. As I mentioned earlier, watch and pay attention to your audience.

Be present. Nothing else matters when you begin a presentation. Your text messages can wait. The leak in your bathroom sink will still be dripping when you are done. The only thought in your mind should be this time and this place. These people. This room. Allow the here-and-now to permeate all your thoughts. Take it all in.

LISTEN to your instincts. The mental readiness to walk before the audience is not just an act of "positive thinking." It is an opportunity to put their predispositions under your control. You must walk out there and do your thing, so why not work a little magic on yourself? When I was in trial, it could have ended up being the worst show I had ever done, and my client may ultimately have been convicted, but I always opened with a smile. I am always prepared for victory.

When you know the material you are presenting, you are the only expert in the room. Take solace in the fact that only you are prepared to share what you are presenting, and no one can take that away from you. Let your instinct take over and do not retreat.

Always **OBSERVE** your audience. We will talk soon about the art of listening, but for now I want to point out one simple thing: While the lawyer must remain in control at all times, he must also listen to every question and answer as if it is the most important information he will ever hear. Each word can change the direction of a trial. If you miss the golden ring, the carousel may never come around again.

If you are willing to keep your thoughts clear and your mind open, you will be more receptive to the information you learn from the audience. Listen and observe.

Let your instinct take over and do not retreat.

As a presenter, watching your audience to make sure that they are listening and staying with you is the one task that can keep you on track. When someone drones on and ignores the audience, the audience becomes far more distant. As you watch, look to see if everyone is with you, and make sure that you're keeping their attention. A well-placed glance to a spectator, or a remark directed toward an individual who is drifting away, could change the tone of your presentation. Thus, your conversation with the audience, and the audience working in harmony with you, can be the best or the worst part of your time on stage. Harmony is far more common when you speak *with* people rather than *at* people; sharing with them rather than lecturing at them.

You can never **REHEARSE** long enough or hard enough. Rehearse your words and actions until they are second nature. Know the details of your story so well that you can jump in at any point and tell your story. If you are pitching a food product, know the taste as you speak. If you are discussing a business plan, know it so well that your mind has already seen it in action. If you are talking to employees, visualize them following your instructions until you cannot imagine otherwise.

In your preparations, rehearse until you can see the result clearly and until it becomes second nature. Football teams do not just show up on Sundays to play ball, and successful presenters do not just show up and rock the house. Practice makes perfect.

SHARING YOUR STORY

Once you have allowed yourself to enter your world of imagination, it is time to extend an invitation to the spectators. You cannot invite someone into your home when you are not there. You can tell them "to go ahead in," but you cannot truly welcome them into your abode. Therefore, you must put yourself in the place you want the audience to visit. Now you can begin to share your world and share your story. I see *storytelling* as a misnomer. I prefer to think of it as *storysharing*.

To successfully tell your story you must follow each of the following steps.

You must **CONNECT** with the audience. Whether you are hitting them with a funny line, or sharing a piece of yourself through introductory remarks, you must create a bond. You must connect with the audience.

Practice makes perfect.

In trial, the connection can be formed with a simple statement or the way we walk towards the jury to begin speaking;

but ultimately, the trial lawyer only has his demeanor and attitude. As a mystery performer, we have cool props and toys that can punch the audience and get their attention. Maybe you can use cool props, or maybe, like the trial lawyer, you can only use your words and your body. Either way, the connection must be made.

I once tried a case where I watched as the connection between presenter and viewer was hopelessly lost. My opponent drifted out to sea, and the lawyer in me was happy. The human being and performer made me want to jump up and fix opposing counsel's failures; but as an adversary, I did not do so.

The trial was a simple robbery. My opening was brief and succinct. A simple statement of "This is what you are going to hear, and these are the witnesses who will tell you."

Since I was a prosecutor at the time, I went first. The defense lawyer rose and began to speak. She wove her tale and did it well. Then she began to speak badly of my case and me. She told the jury what to expect my failures to be. I allowed her to continue without objection.

She violated a rule: She was arguing. I did not object; instead I watched silently, and one by one, no less than four jurors looked at me as if to ask, "Are you just going to take that?"

I politely smiled and nodded at each with a look that conveyed the message, "No big deal." Had she remained focused on introducing herself and her message, the audience—the jury—may have bonded with her as they did with me. She did not follow the rules, and they held it against her. The jury—by jumping to a decision in the early phase—did not follow the rules either, but they had the power. That jury—just like your next audience—were people who deserved or who needed to feel connected to the presenter.

Your audience is in control, and you will connect with them when they feel that you have earned it. A little respect goes a long way toward making that happen.

Those four jurors, with a simple nod, became **INVOLVED** in the case. They were looking to defend <u>ME</u>. They had a dog in the race now, they were part of the fight, and they were in my corner. She gave them to me. I gave the jury respect and let them know they had power. I had not yet presented a shred of evidence, and the jury was invested in my effort. I had already won.

**Make the audience want to be involved
in your success or failure.**

This moment made it clear that these were people with whom I could relate. What a great moment.

An involved audience is with us in both time and place. We must keep control. I used the above example of the wayward lawyer because it was an obvious example of an audience that was no longer "with" the presenter but thinking ahead of and beyond the presenter seeking to meet the challenge. This is the inevitable result of challenging the audience to catch you; they will now chase you rather than walk at your side.

Do not allow a challenge to create a distance between you and your public. Instead, take them by the hand and involve them in your words. Any challenge you make to draw them in must be directed inward. Make the audience want to be involved in your success or failure.

Once you have taken their hand, **RELATE** to them. Make them want to stay by your side. My grandfather, Sherry O'Brien, was the stadium announcer at Shibe Park (later Connie Mack Stadium) for the Philadelphia Athletics. As an announcer, he imagined that his role was to keep the seats filled. Sure, people came to see the games, but he believed that he owed it to the fans to keep them fully aware of the events, and would talk on the PA system to the entire stadium just as he would speak to any one individual. His ability to relate to people he could not see from the dugout was founded in his imagination that they were right in front of him. His ability to relate with his audience is what earned him status as a sports radio pioneer.

Talk to your audience. Make eye contact with the audience. Maybe even give them a smile, but always relate. Once you accomplish this, your presentation will be more natural. Talk to them as you would talk to a friend.

The ability to relate is for some a fortunate consequence of likability. For others, likability can be pure artifice when you are otherwise contemptible and arrogant; this is truer of the legal profession than the entertainment profession, but it is nonetheless a concern.

You are not born likeable. It is a character trait that develops differently in each of us, but it can always be learned. Looking back on my discussion of Ethos, we return to the question of what is it that you are doing when someone smiles or otherwise expresses approval.

The answer to that question is the genesis of your road to creating the ability to relate. An enjoyable benefit of being able to relate to your audience is that you will sleep better knowing that their applause was for you. It will be your success and ability that brings their hands together with approval.

Above all else, ask yourself if what you are doing is entertaining. No matter what your audience looks like, no matter who they are, everyone wants to be entertained. **ENTERTAIN** them!

Even in the most serious trials, I will not walk by the opportunity to get a smile or a laugh. Maybe it is a little laugh because I knocked a book off my desk and chuckled at my clumsiness, or it was the chance to elicit an answer that would cause the jury to chuckle. It does not matter how it occurs, but the laugh will help the bond between people grow stronger.

Next to a laugh or a smile, one of the most powerful keys to entertainment is the ability to keep the interest of the viewer. There are very few laughs in a horror movie, but we are nonetheless entertained. This is because the plotline creates tension and we become emotionally involved in the plight of the cast. We keep our own interest on high alert, because we want to know.

If people accept the premise of your story, and they remain interested and go with it, you can keep their attention. If, however, you are droning on with a story that seems interesting to you and no one else, stop it. Re-work the story and get the audience on the same page as you are; you are the author and the storyteller. It's your responsibility to keep them engaged. Test your story on friends and family as often as possible.

So, is there an easy sure-fire answer for you? Is the solution that simple?

Absolutely not, but it would be a great step forward to identify a list of those factors that are never entertaining:

- Aimless Chatter
- Boredom
- Monotony
- Bad Attitude
- Poor Skills
- Many other bad habits that are not "all about" the audience.

Ask yourself: Does your opening contain boredom? Does it illuminate your skills as "the best?" Does your chosen attitude shine through?

Ultimately, the real curtain may go up before you begin, but the invisible curtain that separates you from the audience rises or falls at the conclusion of your opener. How does your opening allow you to Connect, Involve, Relate, and Entertain? Don't just "do the lines;" ask yourself "Why?" You are not just the actor; you are the playwright and the director as well.

You own the story of you. Deliver it proudly and set the stage for all that follows.

IT'S SHOWTIME!

KNOW YOUR SUBJECT

You need to master your subject and comprehend it cold. If you have to think about what you are saying, you will do a disservice to yourself and to your audience. I once gave a presentation using PowerPoint slides, and while the content was well received, my presentation was rated very poorly. In the twenty-five years since, I believe I have found and corrected the error that I made.

In that early presentation, my slides were my outline. Without the slides, I had no roadmap. Therefore, I leaned on the slides and spoke about each one as it appeared on the screen.

A better method is to begin speaking and have the slides come up behind you while you remain focused on your audience. They should have an "aha" moment when each slide appears at the appropriate time.

A friend of mine gave a marketing presentation. His face was animated, and his arms and legs flailed in all directions as he talked about people reaching and pulling for every method they could grab to find a glimmer of success. The audience laughed at his antics. Then, on the screen behind him, appeared a cartoon of an octopus in a suit and tie with all of its legs reaching in multiple directions and sweat coming off its brow. The caption simply said, "I wish I had extra arms."

The cartoon captured the moment perfectly. Accordingly, the slide resulted in an additional laugh. Also, it created a visual that the audience could hold onto to reinforce the idea that being a marketing octopus wasn't a great plan.

Have you laid the groundwork for each slide in your presentation?

In another presentation, I watched as a financial expert spoke to an audience about trends in white-collar crime. At one point, he talked about several types of fraud without mentioning any specific information. He just said, "There are many types of fraud."

The slides were a crutch that eventually destroyed the attention of the audience.

At that moment a list of the seven types of white-collar fraud appeared on the screen behind him. As he went methodically through the list he lost his connection with the audience. They were reading the slide to themselves. They were involved in the slide content and not in the speech. A solution? He should have allowed each one of the seven types of fraud to appear on the screen as he finished speaking about each type. The slide should have supported his words rather than provide his outline.

Unfortunately, he had never given his speech before, and he himself needed to see the slide on the screen to know where he was in his subject matter. If he had absorbed his own seven points and committed them to memory, he could've talked about them without a visual aid. Instead the slides were a crutch that eventually destroyed the attention of the audience. Many got up for coffee and never came back.

BE AUTHENTIC

Know your subject like an expert without copping the attitude of an expert. Know you are the expert, be yourself on stage, and the audience will accept your expertise.

I've watched dynamic speakers become dry, boring accountants during financial seminars. I've watched attorneys emulate their professors as they try to teach law and explain cases and legal issues to a jury, dragging them into a world that was not familiar to them. You want your audience to be able to relate to you and your subject matter as if it were part of *their* world.

Use examples and anecdotes to explain unfamiliar topics. Don't be afraid to tell stories about your own life. Let your audience know that you are a human being. If you are proud of your family, let the audience know. If you have worked in a business like theirs, tell a story about your experience in that industry so that they can understand that you are one of them.

Don't be fake. People will pick up on it and turn on you. Pretend to be someone you're not and they won't believe anything that comes out of your mouth. Allow yourself to be human.

In the beginning of my career as a small-town Pennsylvania prosecutor, a lawyer from Philadelphia stood up to defend his client. He spoke to the jury using big words that he would never use in conversation. He morphed from a regular guy into a highly intellectual law professor in a matter of seconds. I knew this man well, and I knew that he was a regular guy. But when the judge told him to address the jury, he changed into something he was not. He became the epitome of a law professor. At one point during his argument, the foreperson looked to me to see my reaction.

Having also been raised in Philly, but now living in the small town, I was shocked by the attorney's inability to integrate himself into the community. His regular everyday demeanor would have allowed him to shine. I was stunned, and the foreperson could tell.

At the conclusion of his argument, the judge gave me an opportunity to speak. As I stood before the jury I remember thinking to myself, "Imagine that I'm standing on the street in front of the courthouse and I'm talking to people about the case that is going on inside. Talk to the jury and be real." And that's what I did.

Allow yourself to be human.

When I was in law school, I had an opportunity to meet the great attorney Gerry Spence. You might remember him from some famous national litigation in the '70s and '80s. He was one of the most powerful trial lawyers of all time. When I had the opportunity to meet him, I asked him a simple question: "Mr. Spence, when you pick a jury, what do you look for?" He paused and said, "In my backyard I have a log. After a long day I like to sit on that log and look at the mountains. When I pick a jury, I pick jurors who I would like to have sitting next to me on my log." I took that advice to heart.

Every time I address an audience, I speak as if I were sitting in my backyard. I speak as if I were sitting in my happy place addressing people who I want in my happy place. This way, my audience has nothing but my humanity and my smile to connect with. Every presentation must be personal.

KEEP CONTROL

A senior lawyer once advised me that the best way to behave in a courtroom was to follow two simple rules:

1. Treat the courtroom as if it is yours, and control everything that occurs in that courtroom.

2. Never let the judge know that you are in control of his or her courtroom.

No one wants to be controlled. Therefore, it's up to you, the speaker, to maintain control of the room without being obvious. During a graduation ceremony for a local high school, I watched as the principal gave out the diplomas. The rules that he set forth were simple: "Please wait until I've read ten names and then applaud. If anyone makes noise during a list of ten, I will stop until we have silence." As you can imagine, applause occurred on a nonstop basis. Each time it happened, the principal stopped. He stared into the abyss and waited for silence before continuing the list.

The goal of the speaker is to get people to listen with interest.

This happened constantly during a list of hundreds of names. While the process could have been over in about twenty minutes, the ceremony drug on much longer. His tactics may work in a classroom of only thirty students, but he had no authority over the 2,500 parents and families who were excited to watch their children graduate. His classroom method did not resonate with the audience; it did not translate. Instead, I heard people say things like, "When he gets to Danny's name, we're going to make him stop again!" And sure enough, when Danny's name was read, the people behind me went bananas and the principal went silent. Danny's family had ample time to take pictures of him alone on the stage.

Many times, people who take the stage in a corporate setting assume that their title and authority is enough to control the room. It isn't. Sure, the audience may sit in silence out of fear, but the goal of the speaker is to get people to listen with interest. Demanding respect will only get you so far.

The best way to control the room is to write the controls into your script. Make sure that, when you review it, you don't get bored reading it. If you bore yourself, you will certainly bore others. I always recommend recording your rehearsals. By doing this, you get to know exactly how long your speech will take. The last thing you want is to find yourself halfway into your speech and have to slow down because you have nothing left to say. Finishing your talk at thirty minutes and opening the floor to questions it is an absolute relinquishment of control. Conversely, realizing you only have fifteen minutes left and there's another hour of material to cover will send a message of panic. By recording yourself you will understand exactly how long it will take for you to cover the material.

Another benefit of recording is that you will hear your voice raise and lower, and you will hear the jokes you intend to tell in real time. Think of a wave monitor in a hospital, expressing the highs and lows that occur within the human body. As I will mention in the next step, this rhythm is extremely important to your speech, but in the control aspect, it's important because the audience needs to want to follow you. If you flatline, you will lose control and boredom will set in. Just like a song on the radio, the highs and lows add interest.

LISTEN WELL

The new manager walks into the conference room. The staff members look at each other, obviously shocked by his youth.

He tells the staff that he is only instituting one new change: They are going to start an online marketing campaign using LinkedIn.

He tells the staff to update their resumes, and to encourage their customers to provide positive feedback, commentary, and peer endorsements. The group whispers amongst itself.

"What does he mean by peer endorsements?"

"Why are we updating our resumes?"

And finally, a third simply asks, "What is *linked in*?"

Your audience may not share your knowledge and experience. Always remember that, without a shared understanding, communication will fail. Never assume that your listeners listen from the same mental place from which you speak.

MANAGE THE RHYTHM

Trial lawyers are trained to ask questions that allow information to reach the jury in snippets. When a lawyer asks a narrative question, they risk the possibility that the jury will lose interest in the answer.

The fact of the matter is that people have relatively short attention spans. In TV shows and movies, the camera angle changes rather frequently. If it remains focused on one person for too long, the viewer will naturally become distracted. By switching angles, the eyes stay busy and the mind stays engaged.

The average attention span is approximately fifteen to thirty seconds. That's the longest time that you will keep someone's undivided attention. When your presentation is an hour long, you risk losing your audience over 150 times. Once you lose the audience you won't get them back. To keep your audience's attention, you must speak the way they listen. Keep it short and keep it focused.

The average person will forget exactly what you have said within minutes of hearing your message.

Each question a lawyer asks elicits a single answer. A better lawyer will pause at the end of each answer to allow it to sink in. This is the same strategy you should use when you make a presentation. Provide a piece of information. Then pause and let it soak in. Let them hear what you are saying and allow them time to process. If the information you provide is on task, you will stay focused and the audience will follow along with every word you speak.

As I said, the things that you say should be on point. That means that everything you say should have a relevant purpose to further the mission of your presentation. The average person will forget exactly what you have said within minutes of hearing your message. Make sure that every point you make is relatable to the listener.

My mentor, Charlie "Tremendous" Jones, always told his audiences, "You will never remember what I say. Rather, you will remember what you thought when I said it." If the words you speak connect with the audience in a relatable way, they will think about what you said, and apply it to the context of their lives. This allows them to connect the dots and follow along with your presentation.

Jury trials follow a predictable sequence. The attorneys open and present timelines of their cases. Then each attorney brings forth witnesses and solicits information. At the conclusion, the attorneys speak to the jury and argue their positions. Emulating this sequence—this rhythm—will help you create powerful presentations.

Purpose

Always begin with the purpose. In a jury trial, our mission is to get the verdict that we want. Our purpose is to gain conviction or acquittal. Look at your presentation and summarize for yourself what it is that you want your audience to learn. At the outset, if you can make this overview clear to yourself, you will be ahead of the game when it comes to making it clear to the audience. Once you have defined your purpose, review your mission and all that you are preparing to say to make sure that everything is in alignment with that purpose.

Give Them Directions

Don't address the audience without letting them know where they're going. You do not need to go into detail, nor do you need to review every facet of your speech. But you do need to give them an overview. Paint them a big picture. Give them a 30,000-foot view. As a trial lawyer I always open to the jury by telling them what witnesses they will hear from and telling them what I will call each witness to say. This way the audience can connect each bit of testimony with the summary that they heard in the beginning. It makes the moment more relevant and more purposeful.

Stay the Course

You have given the audience your overview, but now you must follow that roadmap so that they can come along with you. By obeying your own internal GPS, you can follow the roadmap from the start of your talk to its finish, and the audience will come along for the ride.

Bring it Home

End with a clear and succinct summary of your main points. You do not need to do another outline, but you should hammer home the purposeful statement with which you began the speech so that the audience can mentally summarize the message that you presented. Make it powerful and make it stick.

READY—SET—GO!

It's time for you to deliver your message. You have considered who you are, what you have to communicate, and the type of listener or listeners who will hear you speak. It is go time. How will you keep the listener's attention? Use all of the tools at your disposal:

1. **Vocal.** Use tone and volume to avoid monotony, and rhythm to keep them listening.

2. **Remaining Stationary vs. Moving About.** In a longer presentation, controlled movement may aid in keeping attention. In short presentations, keeping focus as you stand firmly may enhance the importance of the message.

3. **Props and Visual Aids.** If you hold up a report, use slides, or display a new product, it becomes eye candy to make your presentation more attractive. Everyone has had an experience where someone tries to explain a situation using the salt-and-pepper shakers as people. Using props such as these allows your audience to visualize your example.

4. **Feed Their Heads.** Use vocabulary that they can understand. Give them something their minds can digest and remember. In the boardroom, you will keep their concentration and focus by referring to income trends and future projections. On the sales floor, you will keep their attention by providing positive customer feedback and acknowledging the salespeople who lead the field. On the factory floor, you will build a better relationship by telling them that they have greater production and teamwork than anyone else in the business.

5. **Give Them Something to Remember.** Associate your message with an anchor that already exists in the listener's mind. It may be a comparison to a past experience or a past success. Show them the big

picture. In the boardroom, stock charts, predictions, projections, and sales-trend analyses may do the trick. On the production floor, a simple banner displaying the percentage increase in production will tell the workers exactly what they need to remember.

Listen to your listener before you speak. You will hear volumes.

By weaving together all of these considerations you will create a tapestry that will cover a larger range of listeners. In the event of a one-on-one conversation, a few moments of observation will tell you what you need to say to get them to understand.

Take time to pay attention to your communication process and then listen to your listener before you speak. You will hear volumes.

9

YOUR "CASE IN CHIEF"

WITNESSES AND EVIDENCE

In trial, the term "Case in Chief" refers to the main part of a party's case including arguments for which the party bears the burden of proof. It is where the lawyer supplies the evidence to support his case.

Witnesses are not called at random. Each witness in a trial is called in a precise and set order to create a perfect argument and maintain the interest of the jury.

You always want to call your most personable and knowledgeable witness first. You reserve your most pointed and hardest hitting witness for last. You must leave the jury on a high note. Magic shows are structured the same way: We save our most spellbinding trick for last. Any presentation of any type can—and should—be built on the same principle. Save your hardest-hitting item for last.

In a jury trial, the challenge is the witnesses in the middle. Exactly how to position witnesses and how to control the flow of evidence can be time consuming since it is so critical. The factors used to evaluate witness placement are well suited to the placement of information in your presentation.

Once you have established the message you wish to create, the individual pieces should be evaluated to determine their classification. In preparing for court, I look at the following:

1. The strength of the evidence they offer;
2. How well they will play to the jury; and,
3. Will they provide evidence that will lead to a conclusion?

As a performer, my evaluation process is similar. We must look at each individual piece of information in our talk to determine the strength of the effect, and how well the structure of the information will be received by the audience. Additionally, we need to determine how well the information fits into our overall presentation. Our organizational design is our "witnesses" giving testimony to our ability. *What does the design say to the audience? What does the design add to our overall image? Does our content contribute to the ultimate goal?*

A witness can be absolutely clear about what they saw, but if the witness is another drug dealer, he will not be the easiest person for a jury to believe. On the other hand, the witness can be the most affable and warmest person in the world, but his testimony could be very limited or weak due to his vantage point in relation to the crime.

Secondly, I had to determine how the information would be heard by the jury. When you make a presentation, be aware of the information you share. Make sure you allow the audience an opportunity to digest the information. You can do this by repeating the information or by presenting it in an alternative manner to increase the odds of being understood. You should be consciously aware of how the information plays to the audience. If you offer information that is over their heads, you may never recover their attention.

Another type of witness I see in trial is the one who requires deep thought and expert choreography. This witness may not provide proof of anything but, in conjunction with other witnesses, allows the jury to draw an inference that something is more true than not.

Trial lawyers, in the absence of eyewitnesses or video evidence, rely upon witnesses and the circumstantial evidence they create. A judge I knew years ago defined circumstantial evidence by telling juries "If it walks like a duck, quacks like a duck, and flies like a duck, it's a duck."

When we want to create a conclusion in the mind of the audience, we should allow them to rely on that which they know, or that which they conclude on their own. Doing so will lessen the amount of overt convincing that we must do to succeed and win acceptance, thus winning our argument.

Each of these pieces of circumstantial evidence adds up to create a series of inferences that allow for a single conclusion. I should add that none of these conclusions should be forced upon the listeners. That is an important observation about inferences: The audience must be given time to contemplate the inference and draw "their own" conclusion. If you do not allow contemplation, the inference will be missed as the audience tries to keep up. Take your time and be sure they follow you at every turn. If you lose them, there are no gas stations where they can stop and get directions. You are the only guide they have.

A key to the successful use of circumstantial evidence is that the supporting evidence must make the viewer comfortable. Validity is important, but if the audience does not feel good about accepting the inference, they will reject it. You want to allow them to create the inference. If you force it down their throats, they will reject it and your efforts will be wasted. Remember, you want the audience to accept your "world" freely. If they feel like they were dragged into it kicking and screaming, they will shut down and all arguments may fail.

In law, the concept of *Falsi et uno, Falsi et al* is important: *False in one, false in all.* If the jury finds a witness lied about one thing, they can—and will—reject everything he says. In magic, if they catch one dove-steal or one billet-peek, they will catch them all, or they will think they did. You will lose them into their own reality . . . not yours.

We are most comfortable when an inference depends on our personal experience as well as our observation. People can create unintended inferences that are the result of direct evidence acquired in their lifetimes.

What does your audience expect to see? How can you use it to your advantage?

Conclusions drawn from circumstantial evidence are based on the common sense of the audience and the direct evidence that we present to the audience. Direct evidence is the pieces of evidence that we see, hear, touch, smell, or taste; it is evidence that relies on the senses.

The most important types of direct evidence are things the jury and the audience see and hear. First, sound is valuable direct evidence for the performer. Second, sight is likely to be in the realm of physical evidence and the things we show the audience.

Turning again to the world of the magician, audiences observe the actions of the magician knowing that they will be tricked, but allowing themselves to be enchanted by the performance. As examples—with no words of explanation— a beastly looking saw caused the Hershey Theater audience to gasp when it fell through David Copperfield's midsection; or they watched the dramatic gestures of the legendary Harry Blackstone as he created oohs and aahs when he floated a light bulb throughout the same theater.

The silent presentations in *those* two situations success- fully held attention. People momentarily gasped with belief that Copperfield was halved. Enchanted people oohed as a light bulb floated overhead.

Why did these presentations hold the audience's attention? We accepted the reality that the performers advanced. The audience was comfortable with the inference, and we responded accordingly. We allowed the visual effects to speak for the performers; we chose to be enchanted by what we saw.

The beastly saw and the light bulb are physical evidence. The former instilled terror by the mere sight of it; the latter instilled nothing but an expression that said, "I, as the performer, believe I am making magic happen." In both cases, that was the purpose: To take the audience from the everyday objects of a lightbulb and a buzz saw to a magical place. We followed their leads.

Copperfield's saw was large, noisy, and unusually lit to create an air of horror. We all knew what he was going to do. He was going to cut himself in half. The saw slowly descended. We waited. When the sparks flew and the saw suddenly dropped through him, the change of sound and lights joined with the sudden motion of the saw to create an emotional appeal resulting in gasps, cries, and shock. Everything told us it was coming. He was going to be cut, but it happened faster than we were led to believe it would; the saw sparked and fell quickly. He created an inference that events would happen slowly, and then suddenly took it away creating a physical and emotional reaction. We voluntarily entered his world. We flinched.

Blackstone made us enter his world by taking an ordinary household item and making it do extraordinary things. He took the light bulb from a lamp held by his wife, Gaye. A lamp is the place light bulbs belong, thus we concluded that all was normal. He created a world we could accept because all was as it should be. Then, with soft ambient music and his melodic bass voice, he created a moment of enchantment that caused the audience to want to go for the ride—and we did.

In both of these examples, we may not have attributed true magical powers to the presenter, but we freely and voluntarily entered the worlds they created. They each, as Tolkien said, *"produced a Secondary World into which both designer and spectator can enter, to the satisfaction of their senses while they are inside; but in its purity, it is artistic in desire and purpose."*

**Be sure imagery in your PowerPoint slides
supports the conclusion you present.**

Do you use a PowerPoint presentation or visual objects to enhance your presentation? If so, think about the words the images speak.

- Consider the final conclusion.

- Ensure that the images and eye-candy support your points.

- Avoid images that will distract or cause the audience to go in a direction other than along your path.

- Allow an image to capture their attention as your words speak to their minds. (Do not clutter their thoughts with wordy slides that detract from you.)

Be sure imagery in your PowerPoint slides supports the conclusion you present. As you consider the items you may want or need to exhibit, you will want to organize the display to enhance and augment the organizational structure of your presentation.

ORGANIZATION AND STRUCTURE

In argument theory, each witness provides information to support a different conclusion. Each bit of information is vital to the overall goal, but must stand alone when being presented to the court. Accordingly, the jury scrutinizes each witness and then decides how that witness fits within the overall scheme. When we present witnesses in the proper order, and when each one's testimony has been believed, only then will the jury be in a position to logically and emotionally reach a verdict; all evidence must converge to obtain the desired result.

If we think of a presentation in terms of formal argument structure, the several routines stand alone as parallel arguments. These individual routines must be cohesively strung together to create a successful presentation. When assembled correctly, the routines work in unison to carry the audience toward the finale. Thus, upon arrival at the finale, the audience will be logically and emotionally ready to give you your desired conclusion; all roads should lead to this single point.

Here's an example: An audience volunteer opens a normal book. He reads any word. The performer divines the word. Simple.

The proof occurs with each step. The audience member examines the book. It looks like any other book, normalcy is accepted. The spectator is given free rein to open to any page and pick a word. Again, the "free choice" is supported by normalcy, but is reinforced through reassurances that there was no prearrangement. Last, without apparent relevant questions, the performer divines the word. The conclusion from this series of events is that the performer is mindreading. Sure there could be the conclusion that it is trickery, but if the audience is in your world, they are not going to chase you.

Each step of the process helps carry the argument, and if done well, the spectator will move toward belief. More importantly, if the audience can effortlessly and comfortably resolve all claims and challenges, they will be entertained.

So how is each fact along the route accepted? How does each routine successfully result in an independent argument supporting belief? Have you provided the audience with the entertainment they desire? Are they logically and emotionally prepared to applaud your efforts?

When trial lawyers call witnesses to present a case to the jury, each witness must be analyzed, and their strengths and weaknesses must be considered. Each witness offers something of value to the decision maker. The witness may be a major witness, a person who saw the crime, or the witness may be a minor witness. A minor witness is one who has a smaller point to make, but is nonetheless necessary to sustain your argument.

There are pieces of evidence that are not in question, and there are pieces that will be in dispute. You must reconcile these as you prepare. Every irrelevant piece of evidence must be ignored, each relevant piece of evidence must be emphasized, and all adverse evidence must be minimized.

Once the evaluation is complete, the lawyer must decide where each witness and every piece of evidence must be positioned to present his argument in the best possible light.

If the performer fails to understand what part of his message is or is not in question, he cannot properly position each routine where it is needed in the overall presentation. He must learn to balance the presentation to achieve a successful performance.

Every irrelevant piece of evidence must be ignored, each relevant piece of evidence must be emphasized, and all adverse evidence must be minimized.

In the world of magic, the fact that a box is a box will not be in dispute, but whether or not the box is subject to alterations or tampering—or has trapdoors—is the point magicians need to defend with argument.

The individual pieces of evidence must be arranged in the most effective manner to produce the conclusion that there is no trickery. The irony is that there *is* trickery, so we magicians hold our hands in natural positions to present evidence of normalcy. Thus, we must be able to present moments of deception as being non-deceiving without allowing telltale signs. That is the mastery of sleight of hand, or dare I say, the mastery of deception. For example, if a magician is hiding a coin in the palm of her hand, the magi must learn to hold her hand naturally without drawing attention to the hand. The hand must—through training—look relaxed.

During the earlier part of my career, I was an attorney assigned to investigate Medicaid. White-collar fraud is one of the most tedious forms of investigation known to man. My team spent hours poring over medical and billing records looking for the proverbial needle in a haystack.

In one case, we spent weeks reviewing a doctor's charts to support the belief that he had committed fraud. I will call him *Doctor Jones*. Patients told us they had not received medical treatment, yet they had billings to the Medicaid system. He allegedly submitted invoices for medical procedures he had never performed. We did not know whether the fraud extended beyond the four patients who complained or if it was limited to those four.

After about two weeks of fourteen-hour days, we noticed an interesting fact: some of the medical charts were written in blue ink and others were written in black ink. Otherwise, everything was normal and appeared to be legitimate.

We later learned that his office staff was only permitted to use blue pens. When he created the bogus records, he used black ink. This was his way of distinguishing between reality and fantasy.

Recognition of the similarities between his practice and the various methods of magic theory allowed me to realize that my two careers were not that different. With this education, I developed and found ways to enhance my ability to handle both fraud cases and my understanding of the deceptive arts.

Yes, I hear the voices of those out there questioning the ethics of deception in a presentation. Let's conduct a reality check. When an entrepreneur appears before the Small Business Administration for financing, does he talk of the ways his business will fail? No. When a CEO unleashes her new management strategy to the shareholders, does she show them how and where they could lose money? No.

By no means am I advancing that you should be deceptive. I am suggesting the right and wrong way to share information to succeed. It is up to you to use your powers for good and not for evil.

The big move covers the small move.

The precise and thorough record keeping of Doctor Jones provided cover that allowed him to "steal" for over ten years. Prior to our unit's review, no one in the Department of Welfare ever suspected a problem. The record keeping looked normal. Everyone who reviewed his books saw proof that everything was as it should be. But that was not the case. The detailed records were kept accurately and completely to cover the smaller secretive move of fraud. Prior to my unit's discovery in this case, every welfare auditor had accepted Doctor Jones' secondary world.

What steps do we take to cover the "small moves?"

In another case, we found two sets of patient records in two separate cabinets; each patient file was duplicated and changed for billing. The result of the doctor's second cabinet was a ripple in the secondary world that disrupted the pattern and made his overall world wholly unacceptable. When we saw two blatantly different cabinets with obviously different records, we immediately rejected his world and saw reality; one cabinet was legitimate, the other contained the second set of books.

In a third case, the doctor kept both real and fake records in patient files. He used the same annotations and the same inks. He kept records that were indistinguishable in all respects;

so indistinguishable, in fact, that he himself couldn't distinguish between the real records and the fake. His method was so complex that it was impossible for even him to understand. He could not defend his world, because he had lost track of his own fantasy. The resultant confusion in his office made his world very unwelcoming, and his staff reported him to the authorities. His confusion was his own undoing.

I show these examples as physical embodiments of how being fake manifests itself. If you are not real, the audience will know. But, on the other hand, there are always those points that we don't want to deal with. In politics, this is called "spin."

In business, we don't seek to deceive (at least I hope not!), but we do seek to minimize attention and scrutiny on aspects of our products and services that may not be quite as good as an offering from one of our competitors. Play to the strengths of your topic, and don't make your defenses of its weaknesses so pronounced that they call attention to themselves.

Are your steps to "hide" deficiencies so different from the norm that they are easily recognized? Are your steps so "overdone" that the perfection itself makes the weaknesses obvious?

Play to the strengths of your topic, and don't make your defenses of its weaknesses so pronounced that they call attention to themselves.

THE DEFENSE

My Hands Are Empty

A witness's testimony is challenged by opposing counsel on cross-examination; the purpose of cross-examination is to test the credibility of the information provided by the witnesses. In some cases, a person can be shown to be a liar; in most cases, the objective is to weaken the information and create holes in the argument of opposing counsel.

For magicians the audience will never be given the opportunity to challenge the show or subject the performer to interrogation. In the business and entrepreneurial worlds, you may not be so lucky. When you are in the boardroom, on the sales floor, or making your presentations, you may be subjected to questioning and find a defense necessary. At the least, someone will point out the shortfalls of your presentation as they question your conclusions. Your best defense is a good offense. Make yourself so clear that there is no room for questions.

To talk about how to make a presentation that leaves no room for questions, we have to consider what is in the minds of those people to whom we are speaking. If we start with the assumption that the reason we are presenting to this particular audience is that they need to be moved, then we are the ones charged with creating momentum.

Make yourself so clear that there is no room for questions.

Whether you are making a sales presentation, a managerial strategy presentation, or simply educating people, you have to assume that the audience is in a particular place and it is your job to move them to a new place. In this new place, they have acquired the knowledge you offer.

Accept, for the sake of argument, the proposition that all people are in conflict. That conflict is because they have reached a certain place, and are not going to move forward without external assistance. In order to get them to move from their current position, you must resolve the conflict and allow them to move forward comfortably. If I were to return to the discussion of Aristotle and dead Greek philosophers, I would state that people are in stasis. You as the presenter are the vehicle by which they will move forward and grow. You must create momentum.

If you make your presentation with momentum in mind, you will be much more successful. With that mindset, you will address all of the arguments that one would offer to stay in stasis. Consider that by taking the offensive and knocking out their defenses as part of your master plan, you will achieve your goal to become a master presenter.

There are considerable benefits to such an approach because you will clarify your thoughts and understand your position better after you have prepared for the arguments of others.

When you think about the other person's point of view, you will give consideration to the assumptions and beliefs of the other person, you will do more research, and focus better upon the challenges.

If you are dealing with a larger group, that is where it gets exciting, because as you prepare you have to imagine that not one but 10,000 will attack you. Under those circumstances, you will prepare with much more vigor.

In the end, you will be the expert because you will understand the pros and cons of every point you make. You will have a better understanding of the specific points which are most critical to advance your position. You will learn from your preparation the best arrangement for the information you are going to present.

In late 2017, I bought a car for my daughter. The sales rep was referred to me by a friend whom I greatly respected; therefore, the rep had already earned my respect by virtue of my respect for my friend. The dealership manager approached and said hello. It was at that moment that we realized she was a childhood friend of my wife. She now had our trust. The only thing that these two people needed to do to make a sale was to dispel my lifelong-irrational distrust of car salespersons. They began by explaining the pricing structure, their profit margin, and how the various incentives were applied. We then began negotiations.

The salespeople had already personally proven themselves by virtue of prior contact. I had a positive attitude about the "presenters." The only argument they had to make to get me to move from my fixed position of distrust was to provide me with sufficient facts to conclude that they were going to be honest in the business deal. They started with a clear and focused presentation to assure me that it was safe for me to move, I moved, and we closed a deal. Sure, they gave me information, but the question is, why did I move? I moved because the reputations of the two people providing the information was of high quality. They properly identified the issue in my mind as one of price and value. By openly explaining how they operated, they allayed my fears that in some way this car dealership would take advantage of me. Once they made this determination, they presented me with facts that were directly pointed at my unspoken challenge. I acquiesced and bought a car.

In court, I always knew that my every action and spoken word would be subject to scrutiny, but as a magician, when I took a stage, I knew the audience would not be audibly challenging me. They would either like me or hate me, but they would never question me or challenge my actions out loud (except for the occasional heckler).

If you have the benefit of presenting to a very large crowd that does not have the opportunity to question you, then you have the benefit and joy of speaking without challenge. That makes the larger crowd good news. While I call this good news, it is also bad news; perhaps it is the worst news possible.

Why? Because without having the need to survive scrutiny, it is very easy for a presenter to go through "the motions" without considering the "reason why." When this occurs, the presenter is destined for failure. You should always be willing to address the skeptics with supporting information to mitigate their concerns.

The magician must prove the reality of what he does. Pulling a rabbit out of an empty hat needs to appear magical. It is the manner of the presentation that creates the ambience. Presenters in the business world, much like magicians, must simultaneously convince the rational mind and meet the challenges of the imagination in order to succeed.

If the magician has no argument to make, and if the entire audience agreed that magic was real, he would never have to show his hands empty; it would be an assumption. Assumptions leave holes in presentations.

To prepare your presentation to withstand the unspoken cross examination of the listeners, you must be in control of every detail. If there is a weak point, you must be ready to work either through or around the weakness.

If a lawyer knows a witness will crumble and admit his eyesight is weak, she must certainly be able to present another witness to corroborate the testimony or her whole case will fall. If you recognize a weakness in your presentation, you need to find a secondary example to buttress the weakness. In some situations, the search for the new information will help you realize that the original information is no longer needed and your secondary support will become primary. Thus, you will streamline the presentation and achieve more effective results.

Your unseen opponent is the doubt that dwells in the minds of the spectators. You must be prepared to answer each question the audience might think to ask. No, you will never hear the questions, nor will you be subject to oral scrutiny, but the credibility of your knowledge will be tested by the listeners' resistance to moving.

To prepare your presentation to withstand the unspoken cross examination of the listeners, you must be in control of every detail.

It has been said that the problems that are the worst to deal with are the ones you don't prepare for. The problems you know about are easy to prepare for. You can also work around the ones you can anticipate. You must anticipate doubt and questions. And the worst problems in the world are "the imaginary problems, because you imagine that they are the worst." (Again, thank you, Charlie "Tremendous" Jones.)

As you anticipate the weakness and adjust your perform-ance, your argument will get stronger; your ability to convince will grow with each rehearsal and each performance. You must always strive to improve. As you put effort into your growth and development, you will continue to gain better insight into who you are and what you are doing. With that awareness, you will learn to foresee and address challenges.

By now, I hope you understand why I see a presentation as an argument. You are presenting information to move people from where they are when you begin to where you want them to be when you end. In a true argument—a bilateral argument—there is give and take. In the argument conducted by a presenter, we must pretend there is give and take.

How do you find all the holes in your case? Simple. You commit yourself to endless review and study of the details. You cannot survive an attack unless you have a firm grasp on your entire argument, and all your material. The more you know, the better you will be. If you are going to act as a tour guide, you need to understand that world better than anyone else. Otherwise, you are at the mercy of the audience.

There are four reasons why people stay in their current undecided, immobilized mental state. These are:

- Facts & Conjecture
- Definition
- Quality
- Policy

Let us take a moment to look at each.

Facts & Conjecture

One of the main reasons that people stay in stasis is that they do not have sufficient information to make a decision, thus they resist change. It is up to you as the presenter to tell them what it is they need to know.

You want the audience to find answers to any questions they may have about your topic.

One of the most common mistakes that a young lawyer makes is not asking for a verdict. In the world of sales, for a number of reasons, people don't ask for the sale. People need to be guided through the decision-making process by being told what decision to make. In management, when you try to get people to take action to improve a situation, it is important that you seek their acceptance of your solution. Tell them up front what the decision is going to be, and then provide them with enough information to understand the nature of the problem. Show them what caused the problem, and explain what changes will correct the problem. Once you have done that, you are poised to suggest the best method to correct the problem.

Ultimately, you want the audience to find answers to any questions they may have about your topic. If you make assumptions, they will fill in the blanks with inferences and deductions or guesswork. Their opinion of your content will hinge on the number of guesses they need to make to fill the gaps in their thoughts.

**You may simply be seeking to educate your
audience, but that does not change the fact that
they need to know what they need to know.**

Definition

After sharing the information, summarize the conclusion and
narrow their focus to the conclusions you want them to reach.
Frankly, the greatest successes in the legal world are those
where the lawyer has narrowed the issue to a simple conclusion rather than the legal mumbo-jumbo that exists in court.
In the 1990s "trial of the century," O.J. Simpson was tried for
the murder of his wife and Ron Goldman. In the closing
argument, attorney Johnny Cochran held up a glove from
the crime scene and said, "If the glove doesn't fit, you must
acquit." With this simple rhythmic phrase, Cochran reduced
the decision to an elementary level. As such, everything was
much more understandable to the jury. Even though there are
probably many other factors that went into the jury's decision,
the simplicity of the statement stayed with the jury through
deliberations, because it was easy and memorable.

You may simply be seeking to educate your audience, but
that does not change the fact that they need to know what
they need to know. Tell them where you are taking them so
they can follow you with confidence.

Quality

People want to know the quality of the information you provide. The listeners need to know the information is important. My favorite example of stasis in quality is my fourth-grade class repeatedly asking our math teacher, "Why do we need to know this?"

At that point in our lives, math was not something that we needed to do. We did not pay for groceries, collect paychecks, or worry about stock prices. We saw no need for math.

Our teacher failed to define the quality of the material, so we could not understand why math was important. Neither did we know the severity or consequences of not learning division and multiplication. If we only had understood what would happen if we didn't, or the benefits of actually learning math, we would have paid much more attention in class.

Policy

When you speak to people, focus on the action that needs to be taken. People want to know what steps they need to take to learn from you, and they need to know what action they must take as a result of listening to you. If the audience needs to work with each other, they need to know that. People need to know what has to happen for them to be part of a solution. Tell them what should be done and give them a foundation to embrace the information that you provide.

While you prepare your presentation, and the information that you have amassed becomes clearer to you, you should consider each of these four areas to mobilize your audience into action. Your desired goal may be to teach them, but that growth process requires them to move from their current position to a new, more educated position.

As a trial lawyer, it was always my job to ask for a verdict. A lawyer wants to move people to make a decision. The effective application of each of the above areas of concern becomes clear during preparation. There is always another lawyer asking for the opposite decision. So, as I prepared, I would look to see what the other lawyer was asking for, and what information he would be presenting. So really, I was preparing two cases at the same time. As I think back on my math class, I always keep in mind the question, "Why do we need to know this?" My reason for remembering this question again and again is that the jury mentally asked that question with each witness they heard. "Why is this information important?" I knew that someone else would challenge my assertion that the witness was valuable. By making sure I was the one with the answers to their unspoken questions, I was the person the jury looked to for guidance. In doing so, I was in control of the courtroom and the decision-making process.

Let's look at this analysis using the time-honored magic trick of *pick a card, any card*. When doing a card trick, the challenges I imagine are:

- "The deck is fake."
- "The deck is stacked."
- "You peeked."
- "You are just good with your hands."

First is the challenge that the deck is fake. This argument can be overcome by using facts. The magician thwarts this attack by freely showing the deck before he does the trick.

Next, the imagined challenger may say it is a stacked deck or all the cards are the same. By allowing a review of the faces, the magician assures us of randomness.

The magician will shuffle the cards. He may give someone else the cards to shuffle. Allowing a spectator to shuffle assures onlookers that the deck is randomly mixed.

Third is the "but you peeked" challenge. The effective performer will use body language to loudly shout, "I am not peeking." A turn of the head ever so slightly creates the image that tells the watchers, "I am looking over here … not at the cards." A simple trusting gesture answers this imagined challenge.

Then there is the "Man, you are fast with your hands" issue. To this one, my initial reaction is, who cares? For this challenger there is entertainment in the conclusion that you have skill. This assertion is not that bad of a result. And by the way, as a magician, you should want to be seen as a person with mad skills.

We must learn to imagine the questions and answers; we must allow our imaginations to think beyond our own thinking and see the thinking of our naysayers.

When a trial lawyer foresees a question that concerns her, she waits for the attack. She knows that her client will be asked about his prior record of thefts or will admit to drinking. She prepares for the challenges that she can manage. She may know that there is one challenge that could prove fatal. The lawyer cannot dwell on that question and answer; if she did she would probably collapse from stress.

The same applies to the business presenter. Do not beat yourself up. Do all that you can but recognize the impossibility of beating the impossible. Do your best to accent the other areas of the battle to minimize the effects of the challenger. By working on other aspects of the performance, you will keep your audience grounded in your world and you will succeed overall; losing one battle does not mean you lose the war.

With each argument, we must learn to imagine the questions and answers; we must allow our imaginations to think beyond our own thinking and see the thinking of our naysayers. When we do that we will be more convincing to a watchful and judging audience.

THE CLOSING
ARGUMENT

Bring the Baby Home

In court, the *Closing* is a cohesive summary of all the evidence that supports the belief you seek to instill in the minds of the jury. It is the final impression you leave with them.

In a magic show, it is the final, most impressive illusion. And, in a fireworks display, it is the big climax with the most rockets, explosions, and flashes.

In your presentation, it is your final display of knowledge and your grand exit. Leave them impressed. Leave them better for having met you. And leave them willing to embrace your content as useful, valuable, and necessary.

Ultimately, the closing is your last chance to make a difference. When a racehorse comes around the final turn, the jockey coaxes the horse to change its gait to adopt a winning stride. At that moment, all the horse's training and the jockey's strategy come together. They create one final sprint to the finish. The victory is the culmination of everything for which they have trained. It is the make-or-break moment. They either finish well or they lose.

Sadly, a well-executed and presented argument can end badly if you are not prepared to wrap up all of the points that you made. Weave all you have said into a cohesive package that leads to the conclusion you seek. Be ready to remind the audience why the information matters to them, and why it is important in their lives.

You must carefully consider your closing to ensure that it contains all of the elements that you want your audience to remember, presented in such a way that the audience wants to love you, accept your knowledge, and apply it to their lives.

Many magicians close with an illusion because it's "big" or because it's the most expensive trick they own. Sometimes that can be good, but if the illusion isn't staged correctly or it doesn't send an exciting, engaging message, it was not worth the money the magician spent to buy it.

In my youth, I ended my kid's show with a bunny production. It was cool. It was alive. I began to realize when re-booking venues that the bunny was all the kids remembered (and that he appeared from a box). I would think, *"Hello! Hello? I am the magician. I am over here!"*

Your conclusion is your last opportunity to get your audience to embrace you and your message.

In the search for a new closing, I realized I put too much faith in the box and the bunny. The routine highlighted the wrong part of the effect. The bunny was the star. I needed to be the one they remembered; I was the one who needed to be accepted. Otherwise, I was fungible. I was the same as every other magician with a bunny and a box.

Your conclusion is your last opportunity to get your audience to embrace you and your message. They may need to assimilate your information into their jobs, their personal lives, or other aspects of improvement, but they need to know that. This is your final chance to explain to them why they need to take your words with them and keep what they learned in their hearts and minds.

To effectively make this happen, your conclusion must have four components. These are:

- A summary
- A call to action
- Any final reminder of your connection to them
- A grand finale

The *Summary* is a recap of the main points of your talk. Keep it brief. If possible, limit the key points that you will mention to three. Three is a good number and it is easier for people to grasp. If you can keep your message summarized to three points you will increase the likelihood of the audience remembering your words. Remind them of the theme of your talk, and connect your summary to the objective that you had in the beginning. In the early part of your talk, I suggested that you let them know where the roadmap will take them; now you tell them they have arrived.

What are the three highlights of your speech? How do you want the audience to remember you and your message.

In the *Call to Action*, remind them how this information is going to be useful to them and suggest how they should apply it in their lives. It may be the reiteration of a concept you covered, or it may be a review of how they can implement your ideas.

How will your product make their job easier? How will the education they received be of use in the days ahead? How will the policy you are presenting improve their business operations?

Once you have done the above, remind them of your *Connection* to them. It may be to remind them that you were once in their shoes, or it may be to let them know how the information you shared will improve their lives because you can tell them how it improved yours.

If you have adopted the procedure in your life, how is it going? If you have been using the information you just shared, has it made your life easier?

The *Grand Finale* is that final fireworks display. It is an impactful moment where you will pull them in and drive home your message. There are four main components to a grand finale.

- Be authentic.
- Be clear.
- Be certain.
- Be passionate.

To bring these four goals together, look deep within yourself and make your final remarks radiate from your heart. You were asked or chose to make a presentation because of a certain skill that you had, or certain knowledge you possess. Do not hesitate to embrace that knowledge and drive it home with confidence.

The more succinct and clear your message, the more readily people will walk away remembering the conclusion. In my experience, being passionate is a byproduct of the excitement that comes from summarizing your message and putting your heart and soul into the words that you speak. You want to leave this audience on a high. Share your final thoughts with unwavering confidence in the information you present. Remind yourself of the excitement for the information that led you to become an expert in the area that you just covered. Make your last line an emotionally driven summary or conclusion.

Your final remarks may be encapsulated in a story that you share, a rhetorical question that allows people to answer only with information that they learned from you, a call-back to your opening, or a famous relevant quote that wraps your message in a nice, shiny bow.

Look deep within yourself and make your final remarks radiate from your heart.

Afterword

DELIBERATION & VERDICT

How Did You Do?

You are alone. The presentation is over. There is nothing else you can do to change the pending reaction. You assume your final stance and wait. The spectators will, usually in unison and hopefully without discussion, announce their acceptance or rejection. *Have they been entertained? Have they been educated? Will they make the decision you desire? Do they accept your world?*

Listen. You will know.

The final applause is the immediate collective response to your case. The trial lawyer must wait hours and sometimes days to learn what the jury thinks. Your response will come in moments.

There is good news: In the business world, if you do not perform well, you don't have a client who will actually die or go to prison. You have the opportunity to do better next time. *Or do you?*

A convicted client is never easy to accept. Looking at a person who trusted you with their life, and watching them realize that it is over, and they are likely going to jail, is the most depressing and devastating moment a lawyer can experience.

The only professional moment that comes close to watching a convicted client melt down is watching your business audience reject your proposal or simply refuse to pay attention to the presentation you gave from your heart. There are circumstances in which such a rejection could end your career.

There isn't much that can be said to prepare anyone for the bad. Rejection hurts; learn from it!

I have always joked that in every one of my trials, there were really three trials: the trial I prepared, the trial I conducted, and the trial I should have conducted. As I aged, it was my goal to one day walk out of a courthouse and know that I conducted all three at one time. After thirty years in a courtroom, that day finally came. Everything went as planned, and I would not have done it differently. The feeling that I had was not as exciting as I thought it would be. Instead of elation, I felt frustration. Why? Because I learned less from that trial than I had ever learned before.

Don't be afraid of making mistakes. Be afraid of making mistakes without learning from them. And when you do make a mistake, at least you will know that the true benefit of a mistake is recognizing it the next time that it happens. Make note of your mistakes and correct them.

You must review both the bad and the good of your performances. Take the time to record what you learned from each one. You must be willing to risk your ego and self-image to successfully evaluate yourself. Always be willing to grow. Always be willing to learn.

Always be prepared to present and lead your audience to the world where you want them to be.

When people are willing, and minds are open, the ground is ripe for a successful conclusion.

The skills that you work hard to create will always require maintenance and upkeep. To keep your world intact, you will need to polish your understanding of your field and your business. You must always keep the stories you tell and your skills in mint condition.

The most effective argument is the one in which the participants enjoy being involved. When people are willing, and minds are open, the ground is ripe for a successful conclusion.

As you develop your presentation or your pitch, remember to consider the methods that you will use. Allow the structure of your presentation, the manner of presentation, and your effective presentation skills to effectively advance your world. These are the keys to achieve the attention and learning desired by your audience. Remember, people do not want to be bored.

Spend time with your material. Stay current. Consider how you will approach your audience to welcome them into your world. Consider how you will prove to your audience that your "happy place" is a world they will want to enter on their own. Moreover, be sure that once you have brought them into your world, they will remain with you as long as they feel the excitement of the diversion that entertainment promises.

Ask yourself: Does your presentation successfully create an environment that allows your audience to accept you, believe you, and apply the thoughts you have shared in your presentation? Have you, through a well-thought-out argument, proved your position sufficiently enough that your audience will rise to their feet in applause to say, "Thank you for allowing me to be here?" *Will they buy what you are selling?*

May your presentations and performances become more convincing, more astonishing, and more entertaining. And, through it all, may your audience find your world inviting and friendly, and may they resolve to accept your efforts with well-deserved applause.

I hope that the thoughts that you experienced while reading this book will guide you to a better understanding of what makes your work successful. *I hope each new presentation will improve beyond your last one. I hope, for your sake, it never gets easier. I really hope that you are nervous and afraid every time you stand up to speak in front of others. That fear is what will motivate you to learn, improve, and be the best you can be.*

In the end, when the presentation you wrote, the

presentation you delivered, and the presentation you should have made are all one and the same, congratulations. You have exceeded the dreams and accomplishments of many presenters.

The information in *What's Your Freakin' Point?* serves as a guide to help you be understood, heard, and allow you to make your freakin' point.

That fear is what will motivate you to learn, improve, and be the best you can be.

To help you along your journey as a presenter, I've created a free training package: *Jump Start Your New and Improved Presentation Skills in Under 10 Minutes.* Go here to check it out: www.WhatsYourFreakinPoint.com/gift

If you would like to work with me individually, have me conduct a seminar or keynote, or if you want to share your thoughts, feel free to contact me at Joe@TheMindShark.com

APPENDIX

The leading rule for the lawyer, as for the man of every other calling, is diligence. Leave nothing for to-morrow which can be done to-day.
~ Abraham Lincoln

PRESENTATION WORKSHEET

Get a free pdf of this worksheet at
www.WhatsYourFreakinPoint.com/gift

Date: _____

Topic: _____

<u>PREPARATION</u>

Who is in your audience?

_____

_____

_____

_____

WHY is the audience there? By choice? Is their attendance
mandatory? Would they rather be by the pool?

_____

_____

_____

_____

Did you ever see a presenter WOW this audience?
What did they do? What did they teach?
What stuck out in your mind about their presentation?

_____

_____

_____

_____

What does the audience know about you?

_____

_____

_____

What do you want them to take away from your presentation?

_____

_____

_____

_____

What supporting documents or information will you
show the audience?

_____

_____

_____

_____

What weaknesses or problems need to be overcome for the audience to accept your presentation?

_____

_____

_____

_____

_____

How will you rebut the claims of the "opponent" onlooker?

_____

_____

_____

_____

_____

_____

THE PRESENTATION

What can you share up front to get the audience's attention? *(Will it be a story? Is it facts and figures that will shock them into listening? Do you have a certain perspective that will get them thinking ... or laughing?)*

_____

_____

_____

_____

What does the audience need to know about you?

_____

_____

_____

How will you make the audience adopt your perspective?

_____

_____

_____

_____

List the five main points of your presentation.

Point # 1:

_____

_____

_____

_____

Point # 2:

_____

_____

_____

_____

Point # 3:

_____

_____

_____

_____

Point # 4:

_____

_____

_____

_____

Point # 5:

_____

_____

_____

_____

Consider the order of presentation. Do the points lead from one to the other? Is the order you listed them in the order that makes your point clear?

Go back and renumber the points to see if another order is more organized or more powerful. Can you get rid of two points or merge them together? Can you keep your main points to three?

Maybe. Maybe not. But try to condense. Three is easier for most audiences.

CONCLUSION

Sum up your presentation in less than fifty words.

_____

_____

_____

_____

Sum up your presentation in less than thirty words.

_____

_____

_____

Sum up your presentation in less than twelve words.

_____

_____

_____

_____

What do you want the audience to think when the presentation is over?

_____

_____

_____

_____

_____

What do you want the audience to feel when the presentation is over?

_____

_____

_____

_____

What do you want the audience to believe about you when the presentation is over?

_____

_____

_____

_____

What do you want the audience to DO when the presentation is over?

_____

_____

_____

_____

_____

ACKNOWLEDGMENTS

The myriad people who have assisted me in my career of learning to be an accomplished presenter and performer are far too many to mention. By naming a few, I risk leaving out many others whom I watched and admired as I learned. I must take that risk nonetheless.

Rick Hicks, as a law school professor, taught me to focus my presentations and not be so tangential.

Judge Warren Morgan of the Dauphin County Court of Common Pleas taught me to be succinct and to the point.

Chip Prescott who, as the Dean of Widener School of Law, encouraged me to dissect my presentation skills to create a law school advocacy course.

Jon Stetson, Michael Spremulli, and Marc Salem supported me—and all my crazy ideas—as I reinvented myself on stage through the years.

Bob Fitch, who taught me how to connect with the audience as a whole.

And thank you to Jason Liller for assisting me through the editing and publishing process. I would be remiss if I did not acknowledge Jason for our many years of friendship. Our shared mutual addiction to books fueled my desire to be an author.

Last, and certainly not least, thank you to my family. My wife, Deb, and our daughters, Olivia and Kaela, who were always there to remind me to get to the point. Thank you.

ABOUT THE AUTHOR

JOE CURCILLO is a consultant who helps company leaders engage their teams to enthusiastically achieve any outcome they desire. After practicing law for more than thirty years and managing his own successful law firm, Joe followed his passion for helping people communicate more effectively, and applies it to deliver speeches, training, and executive coaching that enable people to become empowering leaders.

Joe Curcillo earned his JD from Temple University School of Law. During his thirty-year-long legal career, he served as an adjunct professor of law teaching advocacy by developing a hands-on course that uses the art of storytelling as a communication tool. Joe now uses the skills of advocacy, storytelling, and management to guide his clients to be more effective. His work has been published in *Speaker Magazine, Sales & Service Excellence,* and *Pennsylvania Lawyer.*

Joe is also an internationally acclaimed award-winning mentalist entertainer. Using the powers of observation and the skills that he mastered selecting thousands of jurors, Joe "reads the minds" of his audience, stretching the power of perception beyond the imagination.

He resides in Harrisburg, Pennsylvania with his wife, the Honorable Judge Deborah Curcillo, and their daughters, Olivia and Kaela, who are both aspiring young professionals.